A

DELAWARE
DISAPPEARANCE

A

DELAWARE
DISAPPEARANCE

THE RIDDLE OF LITTLE
HORACE MARVIN JR.

BRIAN G. CANNON

THE
History
PRESS

Published by The History Press
Charleston, SC
www.historypress.com

Copyright © 2022 by Brian G. Cannon
All rights reserved

Opposite: *From the* Washington (D.C.) Evening Star.

First published 2022

Manufactured in the United States

ISBN 9781467150989

Library of Congress Control Number: 2021949181

DEDICATION

This book is respectfully dedicated to Louis A. MacMahon.

Born August 5, 1882	Staunton, Virginia
Died January 30, 1936	Alexandria, Virginia
1899–1910	Reporter and editor, *Washington (D.C.) Times*
1910–1916	City editor, *Richmond (VA) Virginian*
1916	War correspondent on the Mexican border
1917–1918	Editor, YMCA *Trench & Camp* newspaper for the War Department
1924	Editor, *Newark (NJ) Press*
1925–1926	Editor, the *Army and Navy Journal*
1926–1936	Editor, *Washington (D.C.) Herald*

The story recounted in this book is almost entirely due to the hundreds of accounts reported in United States and foreign newspapers from March through May 1907. But of all the articles, the contributions of Louis A. MacMahon, an editor and reporter for the *Washington (D.C.) Times* newspaper provided more investigative and meticulous reporting than any other source.

MacMahon made several trips from Washington to Dover and out to the marshlands of Kitts Hummock to find and interview not only the major figures of the story but many of the minor ones as well. His detailed descriptions of the land, the Marvin farm and the effects of this violation of the family on Dr. Marvin himself brought his readers into the story.

Without the record of his reporting, this book would not have been possible.

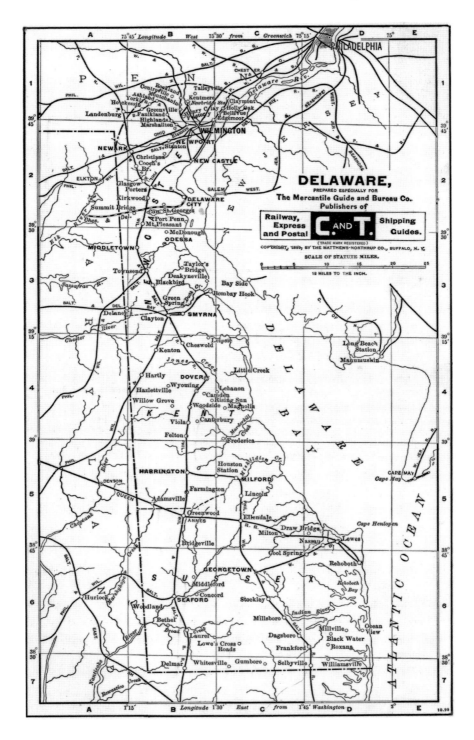

CONTENTS

1. A Step Back in Time   11
2. "I Can't Find Horace!"   26
3. The Family   34
4. Suspects   42
5. "Watch Murphy!"   48
6. The Trail North   56
7. Advertising a Kidnapping   68
8. The Black Hand   79
9. Here, There and Nowhere   86
10. Butler Did It   96
11. "But This Is at My Door."   107
12. Questions   111
13. Judgment   117
14. Epilogue   127

Acknowledgements   137
Notes   139
Bibliography   151
Index   153
About the Author   157

1

A STEP BACK IN TIME

It is March 1907 in the state of Delaware, and a mystery is about to unfold in Kitts Hummock. Now you may well ask, "What, or where, is a Kitts Hummock?" A fair question, as we are about to step back and spend a few months there. Since one hundred years later few residents of Delaware can easily locate Kitts Hummock on a map, and fewer still have ever heard of the true story you are about to read, a bit of background might be in order.

In 2007, one hundred years after our story occurs, a visitor to Kitts Hummock would have found themselves in an unincorporated rural region of Kent County, about three to four square miles in area, southeast of Dover, Delaware. The location is roughly bounded on the east by Delaware Bay, on the west by Delaware Route 9, the south by the St. Jones River and on the north by the Little Creek Wildlife Area. Ranging from a few hundred feet to a mile inland, the land comprises protected wetlands, small ponds and drainage ditches, but west of that are hundreds of acres of timber and rich farmlands, mostly cultivated by large agribusiness.

For a mile or so along the bay and the extensive wetlands of the Ted Harvey Conservation Area and the St. Jones Reserve to the west lies a narrow strip of beach a couple of hundred feet wide that runs about a mile along the shore. Located here are approximately sixty beach homes and cabins, most of which are seasonal escapes for the owners from the heat and traffic to the relatively cool, quiet breezes off the bay.

The name Kitts Hummock is grounded on the English word *hummock*, which dates from the mid-sixteenth century and refers to small hills or mounds along a shore. The meaning of *Kitts* is uncertain but is believed to have been given by an early settler, Jehu Curtis, who in 1738 claimed twenty acres of fast, or dry, land and marsh along the shore. By 1818, successive owners had erected a tavern that briefly occupied the site before being torn down. Then Kitts Hummock became known as a tenting ground for camping and picnicking.[1]

Around 1846, two men named Hutchinson and McIlvaine built a beach hotel they named the Kitts Hummock Hotel; by 1859 there was a bowling saloon nearby.[2] Hutchinson and McIlvaine also planted seed oysters in the bay, hoping to eventually provide the delicacy to their hotel guests. Unfortunately, the oysters failed, and the property changed hands again. It wouldn't be until the late 1860s that it was discovered that the oysters had survived and spread into the bay and commercial harvesting began.

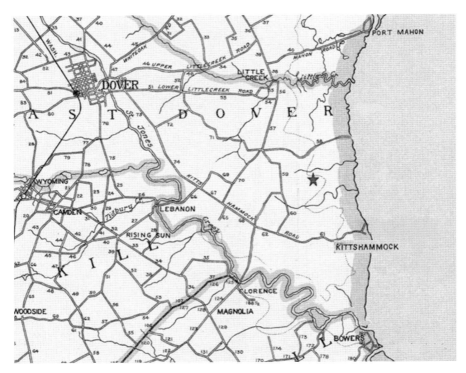

Kitts Hummock, circa 1913. Star indicates approximate location of the Marvin Farm. *Wikimedia Commons*.

First cottages at Kitts Hammock about 1886

Kitts Hummock cottages, circa 1885. *Delaware Public Archives*.

In May 1881, the hotel was leased by Joseph Jeanes, who renamed it the Bay View and intended to "fix it up as a first-class summer resort." The advertising stressed the fresh seafood from the bay, the world-class fishing, board of eight dollars per week, and of course, children could stay for half price. As an encouragement to those people traveling from a distance, if they would send a letter advising of their arrival day, the hotel would pick them up at the Dover train station and provide free transportation to the hotel.[3]

Kitts Hummock wasn't just for visitors. The June 25, 1885 edition of the (Wilmington) *Delaware Gazette and State Journal* reported that the return of warm weather had brought rented carriages loaded down with ladies and gentlemen from Dover going to spend the day at Kitts Hummock until the cool of the evening set in. "The Hammock [*sic*] is a nice place to visit on a sultry afternoon."

About the same time as Jeanes was renovating the old hotel, approximately twenty summer cottages were built on the beach. These were primarily owned by people in Dover, built of simple frame construction of one, one and one-half and two stories, often with wide double doors for ventilation and a covered front porch.

By 1907, the hotel and bowling saloon are gone. Maybe by fire or a storm, but no mention of them appears in the recorded descriptions of Kitts Hummock in our story. It seems from the history of the area, the small local population and the distance from Dover probably served as a deterrent to patrons, and the summer visitors weren't enough to sustain the business. In fact, one hundred years later there were still no gas stations, convenience markets or shopping centers in the immediate area.

Returning to 1907, when our story occurs, the United States is celebrating 131 years of independence and 300 years since the first English settlement at Jamestown, Virginia. There are forty-five states, though Oklahoma will be admitted as number forty-six in November. The country's population is estimated at 96 million, and 1,285,349 new immigrants will enter the United States in 1907—the highest number of immigrants to enter the country in any one year.

Immigration and internal migration have often been sources of friction between the resident and the newcomer in America. Language barriers, differences in customs and religions and often the fear of job loss to outsiders have led to violence. This most often occurred in urban areas where immigrants settled for work in manufacturing or skilled artisan jobs. In Delaware, these types of jobs were primarily located in New Castle County.[4]

In fact, in March 1907, a newspaper article mentions that the Delaware legislature was considering giving the State Board of Agriculture funding to create a marketing campaign to depict the state as a suitable place for immigrant farmers.[5] Two months later, the regional Federal Immigration Commissioner in Baltimore, Maryland, contacted the State Board of Agriculture, stating his office could suggest immigrants settle in Delaware, but his office would have to have assurances on where they would be located and that they would be well paid and receive good treatment.[6] It's unknown if the Federal Immigration Commission directed any significant number of immigrants to Delaware, but the 1910 census totals remained consistent with the previous thirty years of population growth.

In 1907, the president of the United States is Theodore Roosevelt Jr. After taking office as vice president in March 1901, he assumed the presidency just six months later following the assassination of William McKinley and would serve until 1908. As a leader of the Progressive Movement, he championed domestic policies, breaking corporate monopolies, the increased regulation of railroads and improving the quality of food and drugs. Roosevelt made conservation a top priority, establishing the first national parks and forests, intended to preserve the nation's natural resources. In foreign policy, he facilitated the construction of the Panama Canal, which opened in 1914, two years ahead of schedule. Well known as a family man, Roosevelt would have a small role in the soon-to-unfold mystery.

In Delaware, Preston Lea is the fifty-second governor and Isaac T. Parker the lieutenant governor; both would serve until 1909. Lea was a Wilmington businessman and a Republican, but he still managed to secure political support from the rural, and predominately Democratic, voters in the two lower counties of Kent and Sussex. He was a member of the Wilmington Meeting of the Religious Society of Friends, or Quakers, his ancestors arriving in Pennsylvania with William Penn.

Religious friction was rare in Delaware. In 1906, only two denominations had more than 10 percent of the 71,251 total reported congregants: Methodists (46 percent) and Catholic (34 percent). If the Protestant-Episcopal and the Presbyterian numbers are added in, approximately 94 percent of the total number of reported church members are accounted for.[7]

Delaware has a population approaching 200,000 in 1907, divided between the three counties of New Castle, Kent and Sussex. New Castle County had the largest population and includes Wilmington, the largest city in the state. Native-born Caucasians make up 76 percent of the population; foreign-born, 8 percent; and African Americans, 17 percent. At the time, 48 percent of the population live in what was considered urban areas, and most of them would be in Wilmington or New Castle County.[8]

In Kent County, where our mystery will occur, the approximately 33,000 residents would have no statistically significant change in population over the preceding twenty years. Except for the roughly 3,700 residents of Dover, the county was generally rural and agricultural in character.

The rural population of Kent County isn't traveling much in 1907. Farmers and watermen stay close to home. There is regular steamboat passenger service on the Delaware River, south to Lewes or north to New Castle, Wilmington and Philadelphia. In the summer months, shipments of fruits, vegetables and seafood are the usual cargos, with people going on excursions to Cape May, New Jersey.

But the Delaware River is more than a local convenience; it is also a major route for international trade. In 1907, 2.3 million tons of imports entered Philadelphia, and an equal volume of cargo was exported from the river.[9] In addition, the city of Philadelphia is a designated port of immigration, and the federal government has two immigration inspection and quarantine stations on the Delaware River: one at the entrance of the Delaware Bay at Lewes and the second on Reedy Island, about twenty-five miles north of Kitts Hummock.

And of course, there is also the railroad for those who want to travel in a more comfortable style and for farmers who need to quickly get their produce to market. The Delaware Railroad is the major line in the state. It began in Wilmington in the 1850s, where it connected to the Pennsylvania

Railroad and continued south through Dover and Seaford, reaching Delmar on the southern border in 1859. Smaller branch railroads then connected to the Delaware Railroad, serving communities on the Delaware Bay and west to Maryland and the Chesapeake Bay.

By 1907, over 222,000 miles of rail lines traversed the United States, with over 333 miles in Delaware.[10] They reach almost every corner of America and are the primary mover of goods in commerce. There were few citizens of the state who were not within a convenient distance from a railroad station.

For the people in our story, the train station is about a seven-mile carriage ride into Dover. The Pennsylvania Railroad timetable for January 1907 listed nine daily trains to take travelers south, down the Delmarva Peninsula, or north to Wilmington and Philadelphia. A traveler wishing to go from Dover to Jersey City, New Jersey, for example, could take the No. 40 train from Dover at 8:49 a.m. to Philadelphia and arrive at the Broad Street Station at 11:00 a.m. After a layover of an hour and a half, board the No. 74 train to New York City at 12:35 p.m., arriving at Jersey City at 2:46 p.m. All in all, it is a six-hour trip, four and a half without the layover.[11]

Public roads in Delaware haven't changed much since colonial times. In 1907, the state had approximately three thousand miles of public roads, of which less than 3 percent, or ninety miles, were considered improved, or paved, and most of those were in New Castle County. Dirt roads are a way of life in rural Delaware and would remain so for many years. The sight of an automobile is a rarity, especially as there are only 313 registered in the entire state in 1907.[12]

If you need to communicate with friends or family not in the immediate Kitts Hummock neighborhood, the best method is a letter. The domestic letter rate is two cents an ounce, and a postcard is only one cent. The nearest post offices are in Dover, about seven miles away, or Little Creek, about six, depending on where you live.

Of course, since you have had Rural Free Delivery (RFD) to your mailbox since 1902, and you have two mail deliveries per day, you can just put your letter out for pickup six days a week. The railroads carry the mail on special cars, allowing postal employees to sort by destination as they travel. It would be common for a Dover business to mail an order to a Wilmington company and get a same-day reply. Mail arriving in Dover would usually have been presorted in transit for the smaller communities around Dover, and letters for Kitts Hummock would be sent to the Little Creek post office for delivery by your carrier on RFD Route No. 3.

Electricity was known long before Benjamin Franklin flew his kite. The problem was finding an economical way to produce it and apply it to useful applications. Practical electric service in Delaware began in Wilmington in 1883 when a private company contracted with a few local businesses for lights on their property or adjacent streets, replacing the gas and oil lamps then in use.[13] Eventually, it expanded to power streetcars, electric motors for industry and lighting in private homes. But extending electricity to rural areas, especially away from municipal electrical generators, required separate generators, miles of expensive wiring and hundreds of poles to support it, plus an adequate number of subscribers to pay for the service. Expansion of electric service to small communities would be made possible by the rapid improvements in generators and related electrical transmission technology. By 1900, the town of Milford in northern Sussex County had electricity, and Middletown in southern New Castle County started to light some of its streets the following year.

Dover had a city electric service in 1899 and slowly expanded service to communities adjacent to the city. Unfortunately, extending the service to sparsely populated rural areas, like Kitts Hummock, was too expensive without the customer base. The creation of a service to supply all of Kent County was proposed in 1904, but the company failed to meet its commitment. Oil lamps and candles would be the rule in Kitts Hummock in the time of our story.

You have probably heard about the telephone, and may have seen or used one in Dover, but they will not be arriving in the rest of the county for some time. The invention developed slowly after Bell's patent in 1876, with the Bell Telephone Company starting service to Wilmington and the surrounding area in 1882. Local telephone companies only formed after the Bell patent expired in 1893, and Dover businessman and later U.S. senator Harry Richardson started the Dover Telephone Company in 1897. This became part of the regional Diamond State Telephone Company in 1905 and began providing service throughout Kent County—it would one day reach Kitts Hummock.

The oldest, and most widespread, rapid communications network in 1907 is the telegraph. In 1866, just twenty-two years after Samuel Morse developed the idea and sent the first telegraphic message from Baltimore to Washington, D.C., there was an underwater cable to Europe. And in 1903, the first leg of a trans-Pacific cable was in operation to Hawaii. In 1911, telegraph wires and offices were so widespread the *New York Times* sent the first telegraphic message around the world. It took sixteen minutes and thirty seconds.

While the telegraph can send important information around the world, the news is of little use if it is not disseminated to those who need to know about it. That role fell to the newspaper. By 1907, Delaware had over fifty newspapers, including daily and weekly publications; papers with deliberate Democratic, Republican and Independent political views; and papers addressing the interests of particular groups, such as Delaware River boat pilots, fraternal and labor organizations and the Methodist and Protestant Episcopal churches. There was at least one foreign-language paper, the German *Freie Presse*, published in Wilmington every day but Sunday.[14] Newspapers from cities such as Wilmington, Dover and Middletown were routinely sent by rail and mail across the state. And the papers were being read. In the 1900 census, Delaware had a literacy rate over 90 percent.[15]

Many Delaware newspapers had access to stories of events happening around the country and the world. Ordinarily, small newspapers without a large staff of reporters to seek out the news to fill their pages were limited to reproducing local stories or printing secondhand information from other papers. And small communities experiencing newsworthy events had no way to quickly get their news out to other people.

In 1848, several New York City newspapers agreed to create an association to share stories by using the telegraph. Members would have their reporters send stories to the association, which would then make the information available to all the members. The idea was so successful that other associations were formed across the country and around the world, some even employing their own reporters. Soon newspaper articles would mention the Associated Press (AP), the International News Service (INS), United Press Association (UP) and Reuters as the sources of their stories. The individual newspaper editors would take the information provided in the report, referred to as the newswire, and either print it as received or edit the material to fit in the space they might have available.

In our mystery, the telegraph will connect Kitts Hummock with Europe, the North Island of New Zealand and hundreds of communities, and newspapers, in between. The telegraph and the newspaper are the two most important components of our story. Not only will newspapers place, and keep, our mystery in the public eye, but they will also create the only record that allows this story to be told.

Maps

Fig. 7   Marvin Farm Layout (speculation)
Fig. 8   Kitts Hummock area circa 1907 (speculation)
Fig. 9   Kitts Hummock area circa 1907 (speculation)

The Bay Meadow Farmhouse

The only known image of the farmhouse on the Marvin farm is a grainy photograph that appeared in several newspapers and is shown here. The diagram of the house is not to scale.

The house is of frame construction, the left portion being two stories with an attic; the central portion is one story with attic, and the right portion one story with what is probably a loft. An open porch is attached to this section.

The photograph shows the southern elevation, which appears to be the back side of the house, the main entrance being on the farmyard side. There is one visible door in the central section and probably a door into the house from the covered porch. The farmyard side would have had two or three additional entrance doors.

FARM HOUSE OF DR. HORACE MARVIN, SEVEN MILES FROM DOVER, DEL. DR. MARVIN WAS IN THE KITCHEN ON THE MORNING OF MARCH 4 LAST, WHEN HIS 4-YEAR-OLD SON, WHO HAD BEEN PLAYING ONLY A DOZEN RODS AWAY, DIS-APPEARED.

Bay Meadow Farmhouse. *Library of Congress.*

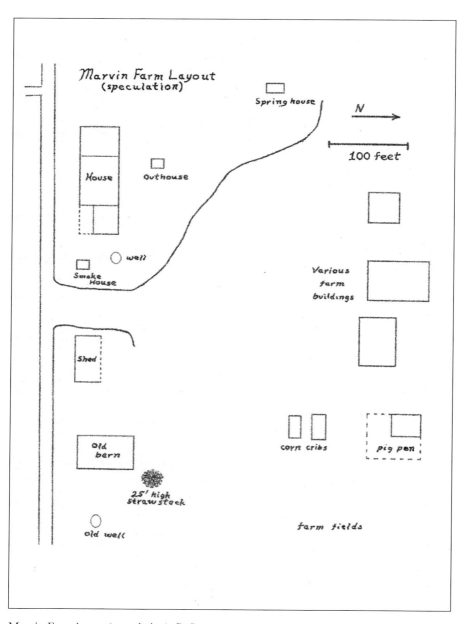

Marvin Farm layout (speculation). *B. Cannon.*

BAY MEADOWS FARM

No credible illustration or description of the Marvin farm is known to exist; however, based on the numerous newspaper accounts that mention the various buildings and their relationship to each other, this drawing is an attempt to give the reader a fair approximation of the farm layout. Farms were seldom identical in design; however, most would have had conveniences for the family nearest the farmhouse. These would have included the outhouse and a well.

Rural areas in Delaware in 1907 did not have public water systems, and wells were dug to tap into groundwater. Volume and quality were always variables, especially in areas near salt water, which often required new wells to be dug. A farm might have several wells around the property, an old well often being left open as a trash pit.

Farms with a spring near the house would frequently have a springhouse. A small, single-room building, often of stone, was built over the spring. The cold water from the spring kept the inside temperature low and served as a cooler before the development of the electric refrigerator.

Another building known to be on the Marvin farm was a smokehouse. This was a small, enclosed outbuilding of masonry or heavy wood construction. Fresh meat or fish would be hung in the building and a small, slow-burning hardwood fire started in a floor firepit, allowing the smoke to circulate for several weeks or months, drying and preserving the contents. At a time of no mechanical refrigeration, this was one easy and efficient method of preserving perishable foods for later use.

The Marvin farm had been operated by the previous owner, Charles Woodall, as a crop farm, raising wheat, corn and peaches for commercial sale to provide income for the family. Buildings in the farmyards would have reflected those used in that type of operation.

Barns are general-purpose agricultural buildings used for storage. There were at least two on the Marvin farm, both of frame construction with an open ground floor and probably a loft.

The reliance on horses for transportation and farm labor required a stable. Similar to a barn, a stable was designed with stalls where domestic animals were sheltered and fed. A corresponding building, the carriage house, would have been near the stable. Constructed to house horse-drawn carriages and the related equipment storage, they were typically open-fronted, single-story buildings, occasionally with built-in stalls.

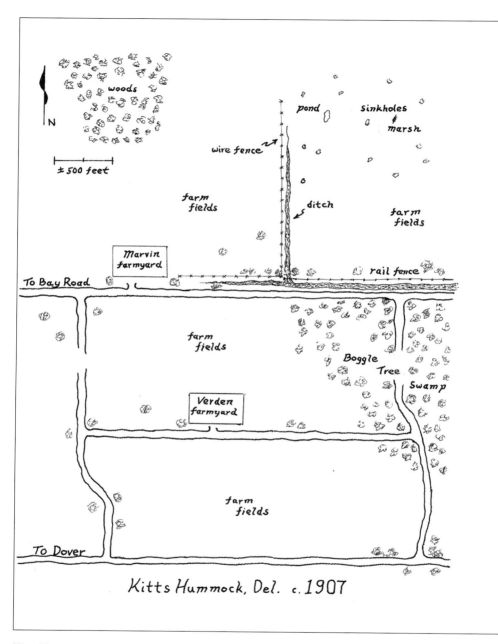

Kitts Hummock area, circa 1907 (speculation). *B. Cannon.*

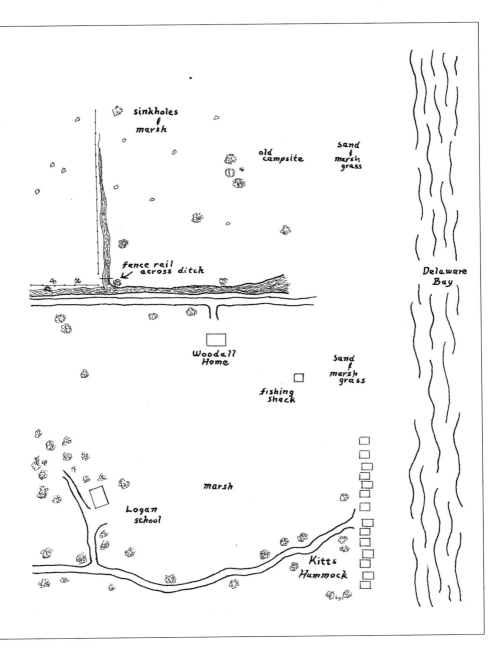

Other general-purpose buildings on the farm, referred to as sheds, were in the farmyard. These were of various sizes, of frame construction, and could be enclosed or open as needed. One shed was mentioned in newspaper reports as being near the Marvin farmhouse.

The corn crib was another common farm structure, consisting of a roofed bin elevated on posts. After the harvest and while still on the cob, corn was placed in the crib, either with or without the husk. The typical corn crib had slats in its walls to allow air to circulate through the corn, allowing it to air dry and helping it stay dry. The slats exposed the corn to pests, so corn cribs were elevated beyond the reach of rodents.

A pig pen is the last structure specifically mentioned as being on the Marvin farm. This was a fenced area, with a small building for shelter, used to keep pigs being raised as livestock. Due to the noise and smell, the pig pen was usually constructed as far away from the farmhouse as practicable.

While not a building, another feature of the Marvin farmyard relevant to the story is a twenty-five-foot-high straw stack located near what was referred to as the old barn. Straw is a byproduct of cereal plants like wheat and rice. After the grain and chaff are removed, the plant stalks are saved and used for various purposes, including food for livestock. In 1874, a machine was developed to collect and tie bundles of straw in the field, but this was too expensive for smaller farmers, who simply collected the straw into large piles to dry.

Kitts Hummock Area, circa 1907

The Kitts Hummock of this story no longer exists. Today a visit to the area would find most of the residents living on, or close to, Kitts Hummock Road between Bayside Drive (Delaware Route 9) and the beach community. The area does have electricity and telephone service, but public water and sewage are still in the future, private wells and septic systems serving the area. There are a few small tracts of land still privately cultivated, but the large farms of 1907 have been given over to state wetlands management or agribusiness. Aerial photos of the region show no traces of the many farm lanes, walking trails, fence lines and hedgerows that once crisscrossed the land and played a role in this story.

The following map shows only features relative to the story and centers on the land of the Marvin farm and farm lane and south to the Kitts Hummock

Road. The distance between these two roads is approximately one mile but is compressed here for space limitations.

The location of the Marvin farm is based on written descriptions made at the time and comparison to period maps. The Logan School was used as a school until the 1920s, when it was sold by the state and became a private dwelling. While it has since been demolished, its original location is known. Other features are based on descriptions given in newspaper accounts and are believed to be as accurate as possible.

2

"I Can't Find Horace!"

O n Monday morning, March 4, 1907, two brothers—four-year-old Horace Marvin Jr. and six-year-old John Marvin—and their six-year-old cousin Rose Standish, were playing around the farmyard of the recently purchased property of the boys' father, Dr. Horace N. Marvin Sr. Dr. Marvin had moved his family to Dover, Delaware, from Sioux City, Iowa, only days before, spending most of the previous two days overseeing the transportation of a railroad carload of his furniture the seven miles from the Dover railroad station to his farm near Kitts Hummock, on the Delaware Bay.

The Marvin family consisted of the doctor, who was twice widowed, his two young sons and an older son, Howard, from his first marriage. A second older son, Harvey, was a rancher still living in Iowa. Flora M. Swift, the widowed mother of Dr. Marvin's recently deceased wife, Ruth, and grandmother of his two youngest boys, had come east to help care for the two young children. There was also Eunice Swift Standish and her daughter Rose. Eunice was the daughter of Flora and the sister of Dr. Marvin's late wife and married to Miles Standish. Standish worked in advertising for a New York publishing firm and was expected in Dover shortly.

For convenience, Dr. Marvin and his family were staying at the Capitol Hotel in Dover. He had made plans to move to the farm on Thursday, February 28, but his family's arrival from Iowa was delayed until Saturday. Dr. Marvin and Howard had spent Saturday night at the house with his young boys and Sunday working in the house unpacking while the boys played outside exploring their new home.

Marvin family collage. *From the* Washington (D.C.) Times.

Dr. Marvin would later describe his two young boys, saying that Johnnie, at five years of age, was a slender, rosy-cheeked, high-spirited youngster, always racing about. Horace, on the other hand, just short of his fourth birthday, was chubby, fair-haired and quiet. Horace was toddling, always liked to have someone with him, and would cry when he was left entirely alone.[16]

Monday morning was the first day everyone would see the farm. The ladies and young Rose arrived about 9:00 a.m., and while the adults began unpacking crates and setting up furniture, the children were playing in the farmyard at the rear of the house. It was an active scene, both in the house and in the yard.

At 9:30 a.m., while the adults were busy inside, Charles Woodall, the previous owner of the farm, and Frank Verden, the owner of an adjacent farm, along with two men, Frank Butler and Horace Caldwell, arrived with three wagons. Woodall still had some personal property left on the farm, including corn and wheat; several bags of wheat chaff, called screenings; and a bag of cork floats used for fishing nets in the Delaware Bay. As the wagons lined up at the barn, the children followed to watch, but their attention was soon drawn to the three straw stacks near an old barn, the largest of which was about twenty-five feet high. Soon the three children were taking up the challenge of climbing to the top, while slipping and sliding and falling into the loose straw.

As the adults were progressing with the house, young John came running in to ask his grandmother to fasten some buttons on his coat. Mrs. Swift quickly handled the grandmotherly duty, and then she and John went outside. Almost immediately, Rose came running in through a back door, looking and yelling for John. She ran through the house for several minutes and, being unsuccessful, returned outside. A few moments later, she returned. "I can't find Horace!" she cried.

Little Horace was the doctor's favorite. Dr. Marvin had doted on the boy since the death of his mother, taking the boy with him as he traveled about Dover, calling him by the nickname "Pete." In a later interview with a reporter, the doctor recalled that day:

I thought my heart would stop beating when [Rose] rushed back saying she couldn't find Horace. I dropped the hammer I held and ran to the stack. Horace was nowhere to be found. Then I went through the barn, the stable, and the storage shed, and I called him, "Oh Pete! Oh Pete!" as loud as I could, but there was only the echo for an answer.

I looked toward the ditch down near the creek, but he was not there. He was dressed in very heavy clothes and being so little, he could not have walked out of sight across the ice-covered bog between the time Rose reported him missing and when I looked for him. I scrambled to the top of the twenty-five-foot stack and looked all over the country for miles around. Down the lane I saw the three wagons rolling. In the rear wagon I saw a number of sacks standing up on end. I rushed madly about the farm and called Pete all the time. I looked under the barn, in the pig pen, in and under my wagons and carriages and everywhere near the house. I thought my mother-in-law would go insane. She screamed and shrieked, "Oh Horace is gone, and we'll never find him here in this strange country."

That remark almost paralyzed me, but I sent my boy Howard out on a hunt and also dispatched a note to Kent County Sheriff Harnett to come out immediately. He did not come out until the next day.

I went back to the stack, examined it thoroughly, but failed to find any track of my baby. I consoled myself with the thought that maybe someone on the wagons had been foolish enough to take him off for a ride. He was an attractive child and looked just like a picture. Everyone was fond of him, and I thought the men had taken a fancy to him.

Those wagons took a peculiar route. They went down my lane to Verden's lane, and up to Verden's house. There, they say, they unloaded the sacks of grain, and put on some wood and a barrel of water. The route they took was most suspicious, and there was no occasion for hauling water two miles to Kitts Hummock when there is plenty of water there.[17] Butler at first said he last saw my baby on the stack and afterwards he said that Horace was on the ground when he drove off. It is all mighty funny....

We hunted for Butler, Woodall, Verden and Caldwell. We found them and talked with them. They said they left him at the stack. Woodall objected to coming back to show the exact spot. I was not impressed with this conduct.[18]

While Dr. Marvin stated he had quickly notified the authorities after confirming the disappearance of his son, the sheriff said he did not get the message until approximately 4:00 p.m. The initial search was conducted by the men who had been on the farm that morning and a few immediate neighbors. Unfortunately, a larger search wasn't begun until sometime in the late afternoon, with sunset occurring around 6:00 p.m.[19] By then, Horace had been missing about six to seven hours. The critical delay wasn't caused by a lack of concern by the county sheriff or state detectives but was rather a product of the public safety system in rural Delaware at the time.

In 1907, Delaware law allowed one sheriff in each of the state's three counties and one constable for each political subdivision within the county. In Delaware, this subdivision was then known as a "hundred," similar to townships in most other states.[20] The authority of Delaware's officers of the courts included arrest of those suspected of committing crimes. However, in a state with fewer than 200,000 people in 1907 and over 40 percent of those living in the largest city, Wilmington, rural Delaware had relatively few serious crimes.

In small towns and farming communities, residents who broke the law were usually easily located and captured. Strangers were quickly noticed, especially if they were operating one of those new machines called automobiles. Anyone who committed a crime had few means of a rapid escape over the predominately poorly maintained dirt roads. And thanks to the telegraph and telephone, even access to the railroad wasn't a guarantee of eluding the law. However, a criminal did have some factors to his advantage.

The position of sheriff in Delaware in 1907 was an elected one, and the constables were by political appointments. Neither office required training or experience; candidates relied on popularity and loyalty to a political party. That's not to imply they were totally inadequate to the demands of the job. But investigating a crime and pursuing suspects were hampered by their lack of training and the time required to complete their court duties. Also, since their employment could end with any election cycle, these officers had to have other sources of income from farms or businesses. They were not always nearby when a crime occurred, nor did they normally have authority outside their county. And as often occurs, local officers of the law who are too close to those who wield power or have control over their jobs may not be as zealous in pursuing some crimes and criminals as others.

By 1891, the Delaware legislature had determined a court officer with statewide authority to investigate and arrest lawbreakers was needed and authorized the position of state detective. This was also a patronage job, appointed by the governor, but there appears to have been some effort to have men with former police experience in the position. By 1907, the state had two detectives: one working out of the city of Wilmington and the second working in Dover. The detective in Wilmington primarily worked for the city police, but both men were under the Delaware Attorney General's Office, which could assign them to investigations as needed.

Unfortunately, while this system provided individuals to perform investigations, there were no provisions for training *how* to perform investigations. This, plus the lack of planning and organization to best utilize the available resources in the event of a major crime, would hamper the Marvin investigation until the very end.

On Tuesday, March 5, the day after Horace went missing, the inquiry began in earnest. Dr. Marvin and his son Howard walked the ice-covered wheat field behind the barn. A half mile to the east, toward the Delaware Bay, they came to a ditch that connected with a smaller one nearby. Both were covered with half-inch-thick ice. A rail fence between the ditches had a rail missing, which lay frozen in the ice, and there were muddy tracks on the ice and the ice-bound rail. The top fence rail was broken, as were the branches on nearby small trees.[21]

Fence rail laid across the frozen ditch. *From the Washington (D.C.) Times.*

The two men continued another half mile east to the shore, stopping at Woodall's house. They asked about Horace, but neither he nor his wife had seen him. Continuing south along the beach to Kitts Hummock, they walked among the deserted small cottages and fishing shacks. Dr. Marvin went to a house he thought might have been a good hiding place. The door was locked, and he could not see anything through the windows. He would later ask Sheriff Harnett to have a deputy check the house, but Harnett claimed he had no authority. It would be several days before every building nearby was inspected for traces of the boy. Despite Dr. Marvin's perception, there were no signs any had been recently occupied.

Marvin later told a reporter that he was sure his son had been in that house. "I tracked the kidnapper there. He was afterwards taken away to some place for safe keeping. I believe I would have Horace with me now if the sheriff had searched the house."[22]

It is important to note that while several people, like Dr. Marvin, expressed their beliefs about where Horace might have been or who might have been responsible for his disappearance, there was no physical evidence to support those beliefs. As would be expected, the emotion of the moment overcame rational thought.

By the end of the week, Attorney General Robert H. Richards and Chief State Detective James L. Hawkins were on the case, with the attorney general taking personal charge of the investigation. A $2,000 reward was approved by the General Assembly and signed by Governor Preston Lea, who also approved employing the Pinkerton Detective Agency to help state detectives locate the boy.

In 1907, there was no national police agency, such as the Federal Bureau of Investigation, to assist state and local governments. There was the United States Secret Service, an agency of the Treasury Department since 1865, but the Secret Service was given the sole mandate of ending the rampant counterfeiting of American currency, not chasing common criminals or even protecting the president.[23] To fill this void, mayors and governors would often give the Pinkerton agents, and other private detectives, police powers to find and arrest criminals within their jurisdictions.

Everyone who was on the farm the morning of the disappearance was soon interviewed to determine their movements, where they had seen Horace and the time between Rose Standish going to the house and the time she returned to the straw stack to find Horace gone. It was a cold morning, and the men loading and removing the belongings of Charles Woodall were working as quickly as possible. Inside the house, the adults were continuing their tasks of uncrating the household goods and trying to get some degree of organization, and the children, always oblivious to time, were enjoying their new playground. The best time estimate was a fifteen-minute window from the last time Horace was seen until Rose returned from the house to find him gone.

The interviews with the family did find one noteworthy point. Flora M. Swift, young Horace's grandmother, mentioned that the evening after he disappeared, she had a dream in which a heavyset, evil-looking man dressed as a fisherman ran from the barn, picked up Horace and ran across the marsh toward the bay. This was taken by Mrs. Swift to mean the child was being held on one of the dozens of fishing and oyster boats that were tied up along the shore due to the weather. The boats were eventually searched, but no sign of the child ever having been on board any of them was found.[24]

The reporters inquiring about the family had heard a story that Mrs. Swift was a spiritualistic medium who went into trances and had prophetic visions. This was quickly denied by Dr. Marvin. Saying that the dreams were of no importance, Marvin attributed the events to the recent death of Swift's daughter and Dr. Marvin's wife, Ruth. According to Marvin, his mother-in-law frequently had nighttime hallucinations, and her "dream following my son's disappearance was probably one of these." Marvin also clearly stated to the reporters, "None of us are spiritualists and we take no stock in visions." The last comment, directed toward spiritualism, was not a chance remark.[25]

On Saturday, March 9, after Dr. Marvin discounted his mother-in-law's dreams, it was learned that she had experienced what was described as an inspiration. While she was holding a pencil, she was "directed" to write "Boat...Horace...Camden, New Jersey." Based on this lead, Dover deputy constable Frederick Murphy was sent to investigate. On Sunday evening, Murphy telephoned State Detective Hawkins to say that the clue produced no information about the boy.

In an abbreviated definition, spiritualism is a religious movement with the belief that spirits of the dead can, and do, communicate with the living through a spirit medium. Even after death, the spirit can continue to develop and can communicate expanded knowledge to the living. It began in the mid-nineteenth century and by 1900 reportedly had millions of followers in the United States and Europe. By the time of our story, spiritualism was seen by many as a fraud and not something to be publicly connected with.[26] However, Dr. Marvin's strong disassociation from the movement is somewhat disingenuous, given that he reportedly traveled from Dover to Wilmington shortly after his son's disappearance to meet with a spirit medium.

3

THE FAMILY

Word of the missing child continued to spread, and on Wednesday morning, dozens of men familiar with the marsh were at Bay Meadows to search it as only local hunters and trappers could. Hunting dogs, including those which had previously traced stray children, were brought in, and Charles Moore, a celebrated Kent County muskrat trapper, was present to lead the dozens of men walking the marsh.[27]

Even the improbable theory of an eagle swooping down and picking up the forty-pound child was not discounted. Two eagle hunters, including the well-known W.J. Honey, came out and found an eagle's nest within two miles of the farmhouse. The nest was inspected with great exertion by Honey, but no trace of any recent occupancy was found.[28]

While the search of the farm was failing to find any clues, the initial questioning of Dr. Marvin's neighbors immediately developed one important lead. A promising interview occurred on Thursday morning with Mary Ann Woodall, the wife of the man who sold his farm to Dr. Marvin. She provided the first tangible information to identify the possible kidnapper and the method of escape.

After moving from their farmhouse, the Woodalls occupied a small house Mr. Woodall had constructed near the shore, approximately half a mile north of the cottages at Kitts Hummock. On Sunday morning, the day before Horace disappeared, Mrs. Woodall had been walking on the shore near her house and saw two people near a deserted beach shack north of the Kitts Hummock cottages that her husband used for fishing. They went in and out of the building several times before going inside to stay. She was quoted in a newspaper account saying, "I was far away, but the forms were outlined against the white beach and I could see them plainly. One looked like a woman."[29]

At the time of Mrs. Woodall's sighting, her husband was about a half a mile away up the marsh road at the Marvin house. When he returned home, she asked if he had been at the shack, to which he replied he had not. She hadn't thought about the incident until after the child disappeared, when it occurred to her that she had possibly seen the kidnappers.

The day after the disappearance, Mr. Woodall went to the shack to investigate his wife's story. He found the door had been broken open, part of the ruffle from a woman's skirt was on the floor and the bed appeared to have been slept in. Interesting enough, despite the freezing temperatures of the nights, there was no trace of a recent fire in the stove. The detectives took this as an indication that the two occupants did not want any visible evidence of their presence to arouse suspicion.

When a newspaperman told Dr. Marvin of the two people in the beach shack, one of whom might have been a woman, he expressed his thoughts on the abduction. His theory of the crime was that the kidnappers had spent Saturday and Sunday in the beach shack, and on Sunday night they sneaked into his barn near the straw stack. In the morning, they watched the children playing in the yard through the cracks in the boards until they had a chance to grab Horace and take him back to the shack. As far as one of the kidnappers being a woman, Marvin felt that "any crook clever enough to plot the stealing of my boy would naturally seek a woman for a co-conspirator, knowing that a woman could best care for so young a child."[30]

Since the evidence pointed toward two people using the beach shack for several days, and no strangers had been seen coming or going to the area, the investigation now shifted to the Delaware Bay. Miles Standish, the husband of Dr. Marvin's deceased wife's sister, finally arrived at the farm on March 7 and, after hearing about the current leads, agreed the kidnappers had used a boat to carry young Horace away. Standish would begin searching the next day to try to find where the boat had been hidden. His first stop would be at the village of Little Creek, off the Delaware Bay about three miles north of Kitts Hummock.

While everyone was trying to digest the promising new leads, a telegram was received from the Maritime Reporting Station on Reedy Island, about twenty-five miles north of Kitts Hummock, near the mouth of the Chesapeake and Delaware Canal. This was one of several reporting stations along the eighty-eight miles of the river from the mouth of the Delaware Bay up to the port of Philadelphia. Operated by the Philadelphia Maritime Exchange, the staff occupied part of the United States Marine Hospital Service Quarantine Station, where they tracked ships and cargoes in transit to and from the port, reporting the information by telegraph for commercial interests in Philadelphia. The operator at the Reedy Island station had apparently heard about the abduction of Horace Marvin and informed authorities about a sighting he thought might be of interest.[31]

Reedy Island Maritime Reporting Station. The station was located in the tower on the left of the building. *Port Penn Area Historical Society.*

Cat-rigged sloop fishing and oyster boats. Built in various styles, some were open, as these are. Others had a partial wood deck toward the bow and often a small cabin near the middle of the boat. *Commercial postcard.*

On Monday, March 4, at 4:00 p.m., a small cat-rigged sloop passed Reedy Island headed north. Ordinarily, such a common craft used by local watermen wouldn't have attracted much interest, but that day the temperature was near freezing and the river was full of ice. The small boat was under sail, the tillerman trying to steer a safe course, while a second man on the bow attempted to keep the large chunks of ice away from the hull by using a long pole. The station operator felt the men in the boat were acting suspiciously; the tillerman turned his back toward the island, and the man on the bow disappeared below decks as if to avoid being seen. The sighting at Reedy Island at 4:00 p.m. would place the boat at Kitts Hummock about the time Horace disappeared six hours earlier. [32]

After the initial search found no trace of Horace, Attorney General Richards looked to other possibilities about who may have committed the abduction. Kidnap for ransom was an obvious first thought. Early in the Marvin investigation, Dr. Marvin had publicly stated his willingness to pay a ransom to have his son returned, and it was expected that someone would soon be in touch with him.

Since the attorney general knew little more about the Marvin family than he read in the papers, his detectives suggested contacting Sioux City and getting any information officials might be able to provide about the family's history while living there. Once the word came back, any thought of an Iowa connection was easily dismissed. By all accounts, Dr. Marvin had been a pillar of the community. He and his late wife had a large medical practice. The family was involved with the community and well liked by all. When word of his leaving became known, the local Sioux City business leaders planned a banquet in his honor, with every important person in the town in attendance. For twenty-five years, the professional, financial and social standing of the Marvin family had been impeccable.

Dr. Marvin would later tell a reporter, "I have never had words with anyone around here or anywhere else. This is something I won't have with anyone, trouble. I never had a lawsuit in my life. No bill was ever presented twice. I have given away thousands of dollars."[33] No one in Iowa would seem to disagree. But who was this cordial, prosperous family man whose young son had just vanished in a remote, sparsely populated farming community on the Delaware Bay?

The police chief of New Castle succinctly told a reporter what people were thinking about the case:

> *Somebody who knows the Marvin family well, it may be some family member that followed the Marvins from the West, will be found to be the persons to throw light on this mystery. Who ever heard of Kitts Hummock until this boy was stolen? Would a stranger, a criminal unknown to the family, ever get an idea of finding a rich family down in that neck of land that you can hardly reach, even when you know where it is? No sir. Somebody who knows the family intimately can tell about this, and when we know if any of the people out there in Sioux City are missing, we will get on the ground floor of this abduction.*[34]

Attorney General Richards needed to learn all he could about the family before he could solve this mystery.

Horace Newell Marvin's success had not been easy. He was born on September 17, 1845, in Wellsville, Ohio. His father, Horace Marvin Sr., was one of the early homeopathic physicians in the area. In 1861, young Horace, now sixteen years old, attended Fredonia Academy, in Fredonia, New York, and in 1865 began studying homeopathic medicine at Hahnemann College in Chicago. He attended periodically, not an unusual practice at the time, graduating in 1883.[35]

Marvin married Hanna M. Fletcher in 1868 while taking a break from school, and they moved to Wisconsin. Within a few years, Dr. Marvin had managed to build a fortune, reported to be $100,000, in the timber industry, only to lose it to grifters in 1871.

Leaving the timber business, Horace and Hanna moved to Sioux City, Iowa, when that was just a small settlement on the Missouri River. Marvin's father had relocated there a few years earlier, and the young Dr. Marvin and his wife settled into the growing community. The doctor opened a medical practice, and his family grew with two sons, Harvey (1880) and Howard (1883). Over time, he even managed to buy and sell a few pieces of land, which led to his second fortune in real estate. Unfortunately, his circumstances were about to change again.

Between 1870 and 1890, Sioux City's population grew from 3,400 to almost 38,000, but the rapid expansion created an economic bubble that finally burst in 1893. Men like Dr. Marvin lost heavily. He was forced to sell everything he could, including a large home he had built, at a financial loss. To add to his misfortune, his wife, Hanna, who had been in declining health over the past few years, died. Now he was forced to rely on his medical practice to support himself and his two sons, ages ten and thirteen.

Within a few years of his Sioux City troubles, Dr. Marvin met Ruth Swift in Yankton, South Dakota. They were married in September 1896 and settled in Sioux City. His wife graduated from medical school a few years later, and the couple set up their practice under the name "H.N. & Ruth Marvin, MDs." The practice did well, with Mrs. Marvin traveling across the state to see her patients. Dr. Marvin purchased a ranch, and the practice was successful; his two sons were settled and doing well in South Dakota. Harvey had also become a doctor but was primarily involved in cattle ranching. Howard lived on the farm with his father and stepmother. The doctor's life had seemingly recovered from the tribulations of the past few years.

The Marvin family grew with the birth of a son, John Swift Marvin, on May 5, 1901, and two years later, on May 4, 1903, a second son, Horace Newell Marvin Jr., arrived. By Dr. Marvin's own account, "Both children were beautiful. They had their mother's fair face and large blue eyes. Our home was a bright and happy one."[36]

In 1905, Ruth Marvin began experiencing heart problems, and her health began a slow decline. Her husband attributed the trouble to the Iowa climate and altitude, and he began looking for someplace healthier for her. Early in 1906, he decided the lowlands and sea air would be the perfect place to relocate his family, and after researching possible locations, he traveled to Dover, Delaware, to look at some farms.

Marvin remained in Dover for several weeks before returning to Sioux City, unfortunately finding his wife's condition rapidly deteriorating. She was an invalid from July until her death in November 1906. Shortly after the loss of his wife, his young son Horace also began to show effects of climate. This convinced Dr. Marvin to make the move to Delaware.[37] He returned to Dover on February 16, 1907, and took up rooms at the Capitol Hotel. With him were his two young boys, John and Horace; older son Howard and his wife, Emma; and his mother-in-law, Flora Swift.

As soon as his family was settled in at the hotel, Dr. Marvin visited the real estate firm of Clark & Son. He had previously looked at several farms and likely discussed what farms might still be on the market from his visit a year earlier. The doctor had also expanded his search for the type of farmland he was looking to purchase. According to a Marshalltown, Iowa newspaper account, when he returned to Sioux City from his first visit to Dover, Dr. Marvin's description of cheap land and the possibility of cultivating marketable quantities of fruit and other crops made an impression on his farming friends.[38]

On February 23, Marvin rode out to the Kitts Hummock area on the Delaware Bay. The previous year, he had seen one of the largest farms in Delaware, consisting of over 570 acres of land, and while it bordered on the bay, it was not as swampy as most of the neighborhood.

Marvin spoke with the owner, Charles Woodall. The doctor had probably learned from the sales agent that Woodall was anxious to sell the farm. Four months earlier, in October 1906, Woodall's thirteen-year-old son Benjamin was taking a horse into the stable. As he walked by the stall of a colt, the young animal was apparently startled and kicked the boy in the head. He fell to the floor and was trampled to death, receiving grievous head and body wounds. Woodall's wife, Mary Ann, was so affected by the loss of their son that her mind was, as described by her husband, seriously disturbed. Woodall wanted to sell the property so they could get away from the memories connected to the farm.

By Dr. Marvin's account, he asked Woodall the price of the farm. "He said seven-thousand dollars. I made no attempt to trim his price a single dollar. He said he wanted eight-hundred dollars for the personal effects. They were scarcely worth that much, but I paid it because I wanted the farm." The sale was consummated by payment of $1,000 down and the deed registered the same day.[39]

The land was identified on the deed as lying on the east side of the public road leading from Little Creek Landing to Kitts Hummock, adjoining lands of Charles W. Lord and James Lord, lands late of Thomas Pickering and lands of others, extending back from the said public road to the shore of the Delaware Bay and containing 573 acres of land and marsh. Dr. Marvin

THE RIDDLE OF LITTLE HORACE MARVIN JR.

named the farm "Bay Meadows." While Charles and Mary Ann Woodall were the sellers, the purchaser was registered as <u>Harvey</u> W. Marvin, not Dr. Horace N. Marvin.[40]

The selling price was $7,000, plus the assumption of two mortgages, totaling $4,550. It's unknown how much remained due on the mortgages. There was also a widow's dower,[41] estimated to be around $2,500. According to Dr. Marvin's account to the *Washington Times*, he paid Woodall $1,800 on April 1, 1907, which was the remainder of his share in the farm and the $800 for the personal effects.

4

SUSPECTS

As the days passed following Horace Marvin's disappearance, Dr. Marvin began receiving increasing numbers of letters and telegrams. Some offered sympathy, others possible leads on the location of the child. However, the state detectives, now joined by the Pinkerton men, believed some of the correspondence might be from the kidnappers themselves. Dr. Marvin had flatly denied any such communication but also said that, even if he had been contacted, he might not wish to make it known.

On Friday, March 8, just four days after the disappearance of Horace, the Wilmington *Evening Journal* published a summary of the clues that had been generated thus far. The general belief was that the child was stolen by a man and a woman, with the woman disguised in the clothing of a man. They were believed to have hidden in a deserted cabin on the Marvin farm until the opportunity arose for them to grab the child, when they escaped to a waiting boat. A mysterious sloop was seen later that day sailing past Reedy Island, approximately twenty miles north of Kitts Hummock, with two people on board, and a connection to the kidnapping was assumed. Dr. Marvin reinforced this belief the next day when he said the sloop had been located off Delaware City, three miles north of Reedy Island, where it tacked across the river toward the desolate, frozen marsh of the Salem River in New Jersey.[42]

The fact that the two individuals were thought to be a man and a woman disguised as a man came from a report by Ollie Pleasanton, the son of a neighbor of Dr. Marvin. Three days before young Horace disappeared, Pleasanton; his father, Frank; and their Black farmhand John spoke with two men walking on the Marvin farm who claimed to be hunting. Pleasanton's suspicions were raised because they were dressed in black coats and trousers, short rubber boots and derby hats, without overcoats. They carried guns but had no dogs, and when Pleasanton asked where their horses were, they avoided answering. The two were more interested in asking about the Marvin farm, hinting they were interested in buying it. When they were asked if they were staying in Kitts Hummock, they said yes. Pleasanton said, "I concluded that they were strangers and had never heard of Kitts Hummock." When the three farmers later heard about the possibility of a man and a woman dressed as a man suspected in the kidnapping, they recalled one of the two men they had spoken to was of slight build, smooth faced and may have been a woman.[43]

The following day, March 9, the same day Dr. Marvin spoke of the elusive boat in Salem, New Jersey newspaper headlines announced the late-night arrest of John Hart, the boat's skipper, then docked in New Castle Harbor. State Detective Hawkins immediately went to New Castle to question Hart, while the reporters in Dover were equally quick to try to discover something about this mysterious man.

John Hart had come to the attention of Dr. Marvin earlier in the week when Joseph Smith, a fisherman living in the town of Magnolia, four miles southwest of Kitts Hummock, called at the farm. Smith said to the doctor, "If it's any use to you, I saw that boat start out in the morning." Smith explained that he had been fishing in St. Jones Creek early on the morning of March 4 when he saw Hart's sloop come out of the mouth of the Murderkill Creek into the Delaware Bay.[44] The mouths of the Murderkill and the St. Jones Creeks are only a few hundred yards apart, separated by the small fishing community of Bowers Beach. Smith said the name of the man at the tiller of that boat was John Hart. Marvin turned the information over to the detectives, who managed to uncover the story of Hart while keeping their investigation away from the eyes of the press.

Hart had a colorful, and somewhat shady, reputation among the residents of the Kent County coastal community. How much of it was deserved, or how much was fact versus tall tale, no one knew, but it was enough to get the interest of those investigating the Marvin disappearance.

For most of the winter of 1906–7, John Hart had been living in a shanty among the reeds and marshgrass on the banks of the Murderkill Creek near Bowers Beach. According to the locals, Hart was at various times an oyster pirate, a scavenger of wrecked boats and a beach comber, and he was considered a man to be trusted in "hazardous enterprises." He had reportedly overseen shanghaied crews on merchant ships and was willing to take chances. He was also a fisherman, but the local watermen tended to avoid him. And Hart had been seen leaving the creek on late-night sails for unknown purposes in his boat, which had the pirate-like name of *John and Anna* and was kept moored nearby.

Since late February, Hart had received several late-evening visits at his shack from a man and a woman. They were obviously strangers to the area, arriving by automobile from the direction of the Dover railroad station, and had to stop to ask directions to Hart's shanty. It was noted to the detectives that the couple arrived at dusk, which prevented a good look at their faces; however, they were told the woman wore a black hat, with feathers.

A few days before Horace Marvin disappeared, Hart had gone to the general store in Bowers Beach. He mentioned that he was going to leave the bay, and when asked when, he said he thought he would go "upriver" Friday. The locals didn't believe Hart was trustworthy enough to be a kidnapper, but he could handle a sailboat that may have been used in the kidnapping. It was probably not lost on the detectives that Friday, March 1, was both the day Dr. Marvin had initially planned to move to Bay Meadows and the day Ollie Pleasanton saw the two strangers on the Marvin farm, one of which, he thought, might have been a woman.[45]

Hart's trip upriver on Friday fit perfectly with two reported sightings in Philadelphia of a child matching the description of Horace. The first was from Walter Winner, who told police he was positive he had seen the boy in the custody of two Black women in a Market Street store on Friday afternoon.

According to Winner, he was walking through a crowded store near Tenth and Market Streets, when "he was attracted by a scene which to him appeared strange and unusual." A white child about four years old was walking between two Black women and appeared confused by his surroundings.

Winner thought the boy was walking willingly with the two women but did not appear to know them. He had not read about the kidnapping and was not suspicious but just thought it odd that the white child should be in the company of the two Black women. He followed them out of the store but soon lost them in the crowd.

When Winner arrived home, he saw a picture of Horace on the front page of the newspaper and instantly recognized the resemblance to the boy he had seen in the store. Winner told the police the boy had been wearing a brown reefer coat and a cap.[46]

The second sighting was from James Dickson, who reported seeing a boy in the arms of a suspicious Black woman on Monday evening, the day of the disappearance. He encountered the woman at Twenty-First and Market Streets when she stopped him and asked the way to Eighteenth and Kater Streets. He directed her to a streetcar, and as she walked away, he noticed her shoes were muddy and she seemed excited.

As with Winner, Dickson claimed no knowledge of the kidnapping until he saw a newspaper later in the day. Once he made the connection, he contacted the authorities in Delaware, who relayed the information to the Philadelphia police. Two detectives were sent to interview Dickson and reportedly came away "much impressed" by his story.[47]

As more newspapers picked up the story of the missing child, the more the public began to see young Horace in every young white child dressed in a dark reefer jacket and red hat. The identifications were weak at best and more often based on common racial and ethnic stereotypes of the period. The Philadelphia sightings, according to the statements of the two men who contacted the police, were based on the thought it was odd that a white child should be in the company of two Black women, or the Black woman with the child had muddy shoes and she seemed excited. These two men had probably seen numerous Black women caring for a white child before, but when the white child might be a kidnap victim, the women were not caring for but abducting the child. This would occur many times during the Marvin investigation and include suspects of Italian, eastern European, Mexican and even American Indian heritage.

The casual connection of an individual with a child who looked like the missing boy went far beyond the filing of a harmless police report. The two Philadelphia sightings previously noted were augmented by a call to the Philadelphia police from the Delaware attorney general, apparently stressing the need to closely follow up on the leads. In the March 10 edition of the *New York Sun*, it was reported that, in response to the sightings, the Philadelphia police had called in reserve officers from every police district in the city and were conducting a house-to-house search in every Black neighborhood.[48] The results produced no evidence of Horace ever having been in any of these neighborhoods.

When Detective Hawkins arrived in New Castle, he found Hart had been arrested late in the evening and placed in a cold, damp cell in the former county jail. Hawkins took Hart from the cell to a more comfortable room and began to closely question him about his recent movements on the river. Hart refuted the idea that he had left Bowers Beach on Monday. The wind was blowing half a gale, and the river was full of ice. Any sailor in a small boat would have been foolhardy to go out. His boat was only twenty-five feet long, and with a twenty-two-inch draft, it would not have fared well against the ice. That's why he left Bowers about 7:00 a.m. Tuesday morning, with a good southwest wind, arriving in New Castle around 3:00 p.m. He was afraid to go farther upriver due to possible heavy ice and wrote to his wife in Camden to tell her of his whereabouts.

Hawkins questioned him about going to the New Jersey shore and the location of the others seen on his boat. Hart denied both accusations, saying he never carried passengers and had not gone to New Jersey. When he was pressed again about passengers, Hart said, "If I had any I must surely have thrown them overboard, because I did not stop on the route and I had none when I reached New Castle."[49]

As to his being seen at the tiller when he passed Reedy Island, Hart said he passed close to the island and wasn't outside the cabin. A later examination of his boat showed that Hart had an extension to the tiller that allowed him to control the boat while remaining inside the cabin.

Hart did offer one eyewitness to his trip. He told Hawkins that he had spoken with Captain Simpson of the watch boat *Protector*. The *Protector* was a privately operated boat that guarded the oyster beds in Delaware Bay from illegal harvesting.

When he arrived off the harbor at Delaware City, Hart had turned his boat into the wind for a moment to slow down so he could see if the harbor there was accessible in case New Castle's was full of ice. He then proceeded directly to New Castle and had been tied up there ever since.

Hart's arrest had apparently been initiated by one New Castle resident, Harry G. Cavanaugh, whose home overlooked the harbor. Cavanaugh was quoted as saying, "I think he came here Monday, and I watched the craft and saw the man tinkering about the boat." When asked later by a reporter, he declined to positively say Hart had arrived on Monday.[50]

After questioning Hart, Hawkins went with him and inspected his boat. He found everything in order and was satisfied that Hart wasn't involved in the disappearance of Horace Marvin. Since he had no charges against him, Hart was released from arrest by New Castle mayor Evan Boyd.

Before Hawkins left, Hart gave him his address as the foot of Jasper Street, in Camden, New Jersey, where he lived with his wife. He assured Hawkins he had never had any problems with the law and had worked as a painter for the Reading Railroad. Hart said he had no immediate plans to leave New Castle until he was sure the ice conditions on the river would allow him to go home.[51]

5

"Watch Murphy!"

March 11 marked a full week after young Horace Marvin's disappearance. In that time, the farm had been searched several times by the neighboring farmers and the Pinkerton detectives, still without uncovering any clue as to the boy's fate. Additional sightings of the boy had been reported in a dozen cities and towns ranging from Boston to Baltimore, but none had proved to have had any connection to the lost child.

The Pinkertons doubted Horace had been taken by kidnappers, believing he was probably dead somewhere on the marsh. No trace of him or his clothing had been found, and most importantly, a week after the disappearance, Dr. Marvin had not received a single ransom demand.

However, that morning an encouraging report reached Dr. Marvin that his son might be in Pittsburgh, Pennsylvania, with the kidnappers under surveillance by the police. Pittsburgh superintendent of police Thomas McQuade reported that late Thursday afternoon, two men, described as "evidently Italians several degrees above the common laborer class," had been seen on a streetcar going from Pittsburgh to Rankin, located about seven miles east of Pittsburgh on the Monongahela River. The streetcar conductor reported the sighting to police, saying the child's appearance was in every detail as that described in newspaper accounts of the kidnapping. The boy's eyes were said to be red from crying, and he seemed unwilling to be with the men.

Superintendent McQuade reported to Delaware authorities that he had two detectives watching the suspects, and rescue of the child could be possible within the next few hours. He needed some additional information from Delaware before an arrest was made. Unfortunately, the child under surveillance proved not to be Horace Marvin.

The interest of the Pittsburgh police in the kidnapping of Horace Marvin was likely due in part to the child being taken to Rankin. The town was reported to have a large Italian community and was considered the headquarters of an Italian criminal secret society, probably the Black Hand.

At the dawn of the twentieth century, the Black Hand was an Italian criminal organization operating in the form of an extortion racket. They generally preyed on the Italian immigrant communities, threatening an individual or business with violence if they did not pay a certain amount of money. The threat was usually sent by letter, signed with the drawing of a black hand or other symbolic image such as a knife or pistol. Occasionally, they would kidnap children, demanding money for their safe return. If the payment wasn't made, the victim, his family or his business would be harmed.

By 1907, the Black Hand had spread to many large and small cities and towns and was known to most Americans by the routine reporting of their activities in newspapers. There doesn't appear to have been a Black Hand organization in Delaware at the time of the Marvin disappearance, but it is interesting that the first newspaper account of the event commented that it was "some black hand [*sic*] letter or demand from professional kidnapers for ransom."[52] The threat of the Black Hand would come up again before the case was closed.

The intense search of the Marvin farm still didn't convince the Pinkertons that the child had been abducted. They pointed out that there were still places that needed to be checked. The twenty-five-foot-high straw stack that had attracted the children that morning had received only a cursory examination. It needed to be totally taken apart to be sure the small boy had not become trapped inside. And there was the old barn next to the straw stack. It was full of loose straw, and the loft was suspected to be the place the kidnappers waited for their chance to grab Horace. Neither the loose straw nor the loft had yet been searched. Even a well near the old barn needed to be pumped out and the mud at the bottom probed. While the searchers were kept busy, the state and private detectives began taking statements from the people who had been on the farm the morning of the disappearance.

Horace Caldwell, one of the men working in the farmyard on Monday, said he thought it was ridiculous to think that the child had been stuffed into a sack and carried away on the wagons:

> *I was one of the men who got the screenings at the old barn, not thirty feet from the straw stack where the children were playing. When we finished loading and started away from the barn the little girl Rose and the boy John had gone into the house. Horace was playing on the straw. No one was with me at the time but Frank Butler. We did not, either of us, go upstairs in the barn, and of course, we do not know whether or not any one was hiding there.*[53]

To show the speed at which something could happen, Caldwell explained that after leaving the barn, he and Butler took the wagon less than two hundred yards to the corn cribs on the Verden farm, where they helped Verden and Woodall finish loading corn. Immediately after, he saw Rose and John come out of the house and go to the straw stack, finding Horace gone.

Frank Butler reinforced Caldwell's observations. He said he saw the two children go to the house. "The little boy was not near us at any time. He got out of sight so quickly that I am sure he was carried away."[54]

The detectives conducted an experiment to determine the time it would take for someone to walk from the straw stack to the beach. It took an hour and ten minutes, with the ground covered most of the way under a foot of water. Unfortunately, the experiment assumed the weather on March 11 was the same as it had been on March 4. That was not the case. The day Horace went missing the marsh was completely frozen over.

By March 12, Dr. Marvin had begun receiving increasing amounts of mail and the first of the ransom demands or expressions of the ability of the writer to serve as an intermediary with the kidnapper. These were almost all summarily dismissed by Marvin and the detectives as bogus; however, occasionally there were letters that had a ring of truth that the writer could affect the return of young Horace.

One such letter was sent by a former Delaware state detective named Francis to Governor Lea. According to Francis, he received a communication from Charles Tannebaum, an operative of the Sheldon Detective Agency in New York City. Tannebaum told Francis that the Sheldon Agency had received a letter from a notorious local criminal known as Big W, claiming to be holding Horace Marvin in Canada. An agent from Sheldon's was to bring $1,000 in gold to a location on the Canadian border, where the child would be turned over to him unharmed.

This Canadian lead was considered by some to be a promising clue; however, the Pinkerton detectives were not among them. They had little regard for the Sheldon Agency and believed this was being done for the free advertising it was generating, which was significant.

There is no indication that Dr. Marvin, or any other responsible party, had agreed to authorizing the $1,000 payment for the Canadian inquiry, but on Monday, March 11, Samuel Sheldon spoke to Charles Tannebaum by long-distance telephone, reporting that he was having success. At the time, Sheldon was in upper New York State near the Canadian border. Three days later, Tannebaum received a telegram from Sheldon saying, "Looks good. Have been waiting at the Broad street station, Philadelphia, for an hour."[55] Tannebaum had no explanation for Sheldon's jumping from Canada to upper New York to Philadelphia other than perhaps the kidnappers had agreed to meet representatives of the Marvin family. Like so many other vague sightings or flimsy clues, this one died a lingering death.

At this point, it is important to emphasize the extent of the investigators working the Marvin disappearance. They included, among others:

- Dr. Marvin and his sons, who were occasionally working leads the doctor had apparently received in the daily mail
- State of Delaware detectives
- Pinkerton detectives hired by the State of Delaware
- Pinkerton detectives hired by Dr. Marvin
- Sheldon Agency detectives hired by the State of Delaware
- Sheldon Agency detectives hired by Dr. Marvin
- individuals like Frederick Murphy, a Kent County deputy constable, employed by Dr. Marvin for his reported detective skills

Almost all the detectives working to find Horace Marvin Jr. were unknown to the people of Dover, the major exception being Kent County deputy constable Frederick Murphy. He was the hometown favorite in Dover, having developed quite a reputation.

Murphy was twenty-eight years old in 1907, born and raised in Dover, graduated from the public school and served in Cuba during the Spanish-American War. He always had a desire to be a detective and wanted to be elected Kent County sheriff. While he actively campaigned in a recent election, he lost but accepted the offer of deputy constable.

Murphy did an adequate job for the citizens of Kent County, but until February 22, 1907, just nine days before the Marvin disappearance, no one appreciated his commitment to his job. On that day, sixteen criminals escaped from the Dover jail, most of whom had been sentenced to long jail terms, and two who were serving life in prison for murder.

As soon as the town was alerted to the escape, the able-bodied men came out, formed a posse and began searching for the fugitives. The attorney general even asked for aid from the state detectives. For Murphy's part, he grabbed two revolvers, described as of "the Western type," and slipped unseen out of town. While the authorities were meeting to lay out a plan to recapture the men, Murphy walked into town and delivered two of them to the town jail. Over the next two days, Murphy would single-handedly bring in most of the remaining men.

When the escape occurred, the two worst criminals, those serving life for murder, managed to evade the searchers by hiding in a remote swamp near the site of Bay Meadows farm. Murphy tracked the pair for two days before locating their hiding place. The men had obtained firearms and were intent on resisting any attempts to return them to jail. As soon as they saw Murphy, they began to fire, and Murphy responded by emptying the contents of his revolvers toward them. In less than a minute, both lay wounded and surrendered to Murphy to avoid being killed. Murphy's reputation had been established. The townsfolk were now saying, "Watch Murphy!"

On the afternoon of little Horace's disappearance, Murphy went to see Dr. Marvin. Standing over six feet tall, with piercing eyes and dark hair, he carried an air of fearlessness and impressed the doctor, who hired him on the spot. Murphy spent the next two days walking across the neighborhood, questioning everyone he could, and on the third day, he disappeared.

A week later, Frederick Murphy reappeared in Dover. He told Dr. Marvin that he traced two men and a woman from South Camden, New Jersey, to Jersey City and on to Mechanicsville, New York. There the trio turned the boy over to a man Murphy believed was an ex-convict. The doctor's son was hidden somewhere near Mechanicsville, and with Murphy being so close on their trail, they had no time to sneak him out of town.[56]

Murphy's investigation seemed to fit with two letters Dr. Marvin had received the evening of March 11. One was from Richard Wilburton of Jersey City, who asked $1,000 for unnamed parties who could promise the safe return of his son. The Jersey City chief of police reported that there was no Richard Wilburton in the city directory, and the police had no information about such a person or any ransom letter.

The second letter was from F.A. Barber of Mechanicsville, who said:

> *There is no doubt that I can give you some information in regard to your kidnapped son. Last Wednesday evening at 10 pm our doorbell rang, and on going to the door there was a man and a woman, with a little boy in the man's arms. He said to me if we would keep them over night he would be glad, as he did not like hotels. He said he wanted to leave on the first train on the* [Boston & Maine Railroad], *which leaves at 5:45 am. toward Boston. We kept them all night, and the man gave me $3.00. It did not occur to us that anything was wrong until I read about your kidnapped boy today.*[57]

For Dr. Marvin, all the clues were literally falling in line. The boat had carried his son from the Kitts Hummock beach up the river to Philadelphia, where the boy was sighted by multiple persons. He was then taken across the river to South Camden, where he had been traced by Murphy, who followed them to Jersey City and on northward to Mechanicsville. It seemed quick action could have his son home in a matter of days.

There are always people who wish to either make money from another person's misfortune or to make light of it, and the Marvin disappearance was no different. On March 13, Dr. Marvin received a letter postmarked from Philadelphia:

> *For $1,000 we will return your boy. Take the money to the entrance to Brandywine Springs Park, Wilmington, Del. There you will find a man with a red handkerchief around his neck. Hand the coin to him and pass on. Don't tell the police, for if you do you will never get him alive. Others will be around to watch you, so don't try any funny business.*
>
> *THE VELVET HAND*

Brandywine Springs Park, Wilmington, Delaware, circa 1907. *Commercial postcard.*

The professional detectives gave no thought to the letter, as it had the same handwriting as several previous letters sent from Delaware. Also, there was no indication of the day or time this payoff was to be conducted, something a kidnapper might want to be sure to include in their ransom note. None of them bothered to go to the park. Dr. Marvin, however, thought it would be worth it if it resulted in the return of his son. He went the next day, March 15.

In 1907, Brandywine Springs Park was a popular amusement park in the Wilmington suburbs, with rides, an ice cream stand, a lake where you could rent boats and even an outdoor theater. Apparently, the "kidnappers" failed to realize that in the month of March, when there was still occasional snowfall and the lake might be frozen over, the park might not have been the best place for a ransom payoff. The only people Dr. Marvin saw were a man selling candy and workers building a new roller-skating rink.[58]

Early in the search for Horace Marvin, his father received many letters sympathizing with him and offering prayers for the safe return of his son. Local churches and religious organizations, such as the Wesley Methodist

Episcopal Church on State Street in Dover, used the Sunday following the disappearance to hold a public prayer meeting to show sympathy for the Marvin family. The Wilmington Methodist Conference followed soon after. At their March 24 meeting, they passed a resolution to Governor Lea to spare no expense to locate and punish those responsible for this act and offered earnest prayers for the child's return.

In early April, a letter from a Pennsylvania writer suggested there be a National Day of Prayer, as was held following the July 2, 1881 shooting of President Garfield. The president lingered for seventy-nine days before succumbing to his injuries on September 19, 1881.

Even individuals offered their spiritual support, such as a woman in New Haven, Connecticut, who said she could return the boy to his family through her prayers. She said that this was a method she had used many times to "restore lost keys, knives and other articles for her friends." But the most folkloric solution came from an unknown man who told Dr. Marvin, "Take a board out of which a knot has fallen. Hold this to your mouth at daybreak and holler through the hole 'Kidnapper, bring back my child.' Say this three times, and the boy will be returned."[59]

6

THE TRAIL NORTH

On March 14, the Pinkertons organized another search of the farm, with forty men walking hand in hand across all the ditches and 200 acres of marshland. Superintendent Dimaio was asked if these multiple searches proved Horace's body wasn't on the grounds. "No indeed," was his response. "The Pinkertons take nothing for granted. We will search in the same way the woods north of the house tomorrow."[60] However, for Dimaio and the Pinkertons, the search was about to take another twist.

James Ratledge, a former state detective who had lived in Kitts Hummock, was quite familiar with the natural features of the area. According to Ratledge, to the south and immediately adjacent to the land owned by Dr. Marvin there was a tract of land known locally as Boggle Tree Swamp. While much of that area was marshland, there were places where the land was dry and rose in small hills, or hummocks, and in one of those hills there was a cave. It was known as Hutchinson's Cave for Albert Hutchinson, a local eccentric who once lived there and made his living by hunting and fishing. Ratledge believed it was still there, large enough to hold two or more persons and, as the entrance was likely covered with vegetation, probably unknown to the numerous people searching the area. Ratledge considered it entirely possible that someone familiar with the existence of the cave and connected to the disappearance of Horace Marvin could have hid the child there until it was safe to remove him from the area. However, once the cave was located and searched, there was no evidence that it had been recently occupied.[61]

Local farmers and Pinkerton detectives searching the farm for young Horace. *From the Albuquerque Evening Citizen.*

Some of the most reassuring words came to Dr. Marvin from former county sheriff John Wharton. Wharton told the doctor that he had lived for twenty-nine years on a neighboring farm, and he knew practically every foot of Marvin's 573 acres. Having assisted the searches of the farm in the days following the disappearance, Wharton was of the opinion that young Horace "is alive, because I am satisfied now he is not on your farm."[62]

Detectives did manage to uncover one interesting item of coincidental information. Around 1905, a young girl named Elsie Smith disappeared from the farm of Dr. Marvin's neighbor Frank Pleasanton. The child had come to the farm from an institution, probably the Home for Friendless and Destitute Children in Wilmington, that was established to care for abused and homeless children. The children were occasionally given to private families as servants and cooks and often experienced more abuse. Poor treatment occasionally led to their running away or returning on their own to be with family or a friend.

A similar case to the Marvin disappearance was reported in the Saturday, November 22, 1902 edition of the Wilmington *Evening Journal*. Tucked away in a small article on page six, under the headline "Small Boy Found Dead," readers were told of "a small boy" who lived with the Slaughter family on their farm near Dover and was found dead by family members the day before. The child was found behind a straw stack, with no marks of violence on the body. The coroner would hold an inquest, but as the paper reported, "the little fellow evidently died from natural causes." The anonymous boy was obtained from a "charitable home" the previous summer. He was reportedly known to be missing since the preceding Saturday, November 15, but not found for six days. It's unlikely the authorities ever tried to seriously locate Elsie Smith—they just assumed she did run away—or if the anonymous boy's death was given anything but a cursory investigation.

When the Canadian inquiry was closing down, the authorities were considering the March 15 report of a Chesapeake Bay oysterman, Captain Scott "Scotty" Clark. While he admitted he had not seen either the boy or his abductors, he did talk to a Black man who had firsthand information.

According to Clark, on Monday, March 11 he was heading down the Chesapeake Bay from the Baltimore area to join the oyster fleet, when he saw what appeared to be a deserted boat on the beach. He noted that the boat was a sloop, more in the design of those used by watermen on the Delaware rather than the Chesapeake Bay. Clark thought it was like the sloop reportedly seen by the Maritime Reporting Station on Reedy Island on the day of Horace Marvin's disappearance, so he stopped to investigate. Going on board, he found the cabin locked, but he forced the door. Inside he found a smoldering fire in the stove and a blue mitten with the finger ends frayed.

Clark walked a mile down the beach to a house occupied by Rufus Thomas, who was also a bay waterman. Thomas said he had been out in his boat when he saw the now abandoned sloop under sail and occupied by a man and woman with a small boy. After beaching the boat, they all walked to Thomas's home, the small boy crying all the time. They stayed briefly at the house, the man asking directions to the nearest trolley station into Baltimore. Thomas said the boy was kept carefully concealed the entire time. Afterward, the three left, walking toward the trolley station that would take them into Baltimore. Clark claimed Thomas had not heard of the kidnapping.[63]

This detailed story produced some excitement among those in Dover who heard it. If Clark's information about the abandoned sloop could be verified, it might explain the identification of Jack Hart's boat passing Reedy Island the day after the abduction. The boat seen by the operator at the Maritime Reporting Station on the day of the abduction with two persons on board was the one found near Baltimore. The operator had simply confused the dates, resulting in a week wasted while the real kidnappers made their escape south by way of the Chesapeake and Delaware Canal. The excitement, and Captain Clark, soon vanished when Dr. Marvin mentioned that he had been told by a Pinkerton that the C&D Canal had been closed for over a month because of ice in the canal and extensive repairs on several locks.

On the morning of Saturday, March 16, several of the Pinkerton men employed by the state left Dover early under the command of Detective Simmons. Their first stop was the Bay Meadows farm, where they picked up Horace Marvin's older brother John and his cousin Rose Standish. They then briefly stopped at the nearby Verden farm before hurrying to Kitts Hummock, approximately three-quarters of a mile away.[64]

Captain Clark's boat had been fiction, but the previous afternoon another black sloop had appeared and was seen by several people off the Kitts Hummock beach. It sailed back and forth for a half an hour, raising and lowering black and white flags as though signaling someone in one of the cottages. Apparently not getting a reply, it turned and set a course across the bay toward New Jersey.

On Friday night, the reporters learned the Pinkertons had concluded that a conspiracy and kidnapping had occurred in the Marvin case, and they were about to make "important arrests." Pinkerton superintendent Dimaio, working for the state, had been given permission to search the cottages at Kitts Hummock. Governor Lea had appointed the Pinkertons as special constables and approved a "John Doe" search warrant allowing them to work as officers of the state. This was twelve days after the child disappeared but was proudly reported by the authorities as "the first systematic search for little Horace that has been instigated in the only town or settlement anywhere near the Marvin home, and not connected to the outer world by either telephone, telegraph or post office."[65]

When the detectives arrived at Kitts Hummock, they had two assignments, first to search every building and surrounding areas for traces of the child or the kidnappers, and second, to set a trap to try to get the people on the black sloop to come ashore so they could be arrested. To bait the trap, the agents were going to have the two children playing in plain sight on the beach. They were told to romp around on the sand and be visible to any boats that might come near the shore.

The building search took about two hours, and none of the approximately twenty buildings were spared, not even the home of Charles Woodall and his wife, which was located a distance away from the beach houses. All closets and cabinets were examined, floors pulled up, poles pushed up chimneys and grappling hooks dropped down wells. The sum of the ransacking was some crusts of dried bread and several torn paper cracker boxes on the floor of one home, none of which was considered significant.

During the search of the marsh and beach, the remains of a recent camp was found hidden from sight behind several cedar trees a few hundred yards from the Marvin farm. Located in a direct line from the straw stack to the beach, there were remains of a fire containing burned letters and footprints leading back and forth between the fire and the beach.[66] It was assumed this was where the kidnappers had been dropped off to observe the activities on the farm and where they had made their escape by boat once they had the boy in custody.

When the search was completed, the detectives took up positions hiding in the high beach grass. Several hours after their arrival, the detectives were joined by a number of journalists who had deduced their location. Simmons ordered all the men to lie down flat in the wet marsh grass and do nothing to give away their presence. They did this from 10:00 a.m. until 4:00 p.m. At 4:00 p.m., one of the Pinkertons with a strong pair of binoculars saw the faint image of an approaching boat. "Everybody quiet now," ordered Simmons. "We'll land them this trip and get the boy."[67]

The shore at Kitts Hummock drops off gradually into the bay, and the sloop was making a slow approach to avoid grounding. When the boat was about five hundred yards off the beach, it was hit by a strong southeasterly wind that almost resulted in it capsizing. The men on the shore kept a close eye on the boat, hoping to identify who was on board and if young Horace might be visible. Unfortunately for the detectives, it appeared the people on the boat had hung strips of canvas or similar material to block their view. At one point, another gust of wind almost blew the sloop over, and Simmons saw the tarred canvas hat being worn by the helmsman.

At one hundred yards off the shore, directly in front of the high grass concealing the men, the sloop lowered its sails. The two children were still on the beach, playing as if nothing was happening. Immediately, the white and black flags seen the previous day were raised and lowered as if sending a signal to a confederate ashore. This was done several times; then the flags were left at the masthead for fifteen minutes, with the glasses of the people on the boat trained directly at the shore. As the sloop was being slowly pushed toward the shallow bottom and those aboard received no reply to their signals, the sails were quickly raised and the craft moved rapidly away toward New Jersey.

Having no way to reach the boat, Simmons and his team left for Dover, except one man, detailed to remain in case there was an attempt at a night landing. He was later joined by three more agents. The night remained quiet, but uncomfortable, the temperature only in the high thirties.[68]

Later Saturday night, the Pinkertons confirmed rumors that they were in communication with the real kidnappers. It was expected their negotiations would have Horace released within thirty hours. Detective Simmons also confirmed that taking the two children to the Kitts Hummock beach was some type of signal to the kidnappers and would be repeated on Sunday.

By Sunday morning, March 17, the plan of the detectives to repeat the activities of the previous day had been altered. The Pinkertons, this time accompanied by the reporters, went to the beach, but the children were allowed to stay at home. This was the first indication of a possible fracture in communications with the kidnappers. The idea was reinforced when, after several hours on the beach, the elusive, black-hulled sloop failed to appear.

One of the detectives, who had apparently spent the night on the beach, reported that the previous evening he had seen the figures of two men walking on the shore a distance to the south, below Kitts Hummock. He started to follow them but had to stop due to darkness.

It was also learned by the press that the Pinkertons had decided they needed their own watercraft to deal with the black sloop. They had acquired not only a sailboat but also a gasoline-powered motorboat and were now patrolling both sides of the Delaware Bay. And since the criminals were apparently using New Jersey as a safe hiding place, New Jersey state detective Frank Lore would be cooperating on leads in that state. Unfortunately, this contact with the kidnappers fell apart, there were no important arrests made and nothing had changed at the end of thirty hours. But it did lead to a working relationship with New Jersey detectives.

In anticipation of arrests being made, telegrams had been sent by the Delaware attorney general to the Sheldon Agency to facilitate the arrest under New Jersey authority and arrange for extradition between Governors

Lea and Stokes. The Delaware Court of Oyer and Terminer[69] could be convened quickly for a trial. It was the popular opinion that if someone were arrested for the kidnapping, it would take a jury about five minutes to reach a verdict. The punishment was death.

While the search of Kitts Hummock was underway, Pinkerton superintendent Dimaio was conducting a long interview with Miles Standish. He was reportedly experienced in publishing and had worked as an advertising and circulation manager. Standish had connections with several New York City newspapers and was obtaining cooperation from many of the East Coast newspapers, as well as others around the country, to advertise about the missing child.[70]

The peculiar sightings of Horace continued around the country, including another one in Philadelphia. On March 16, the detectives in Dover received information from Captain Donaghy of the Philadelphia police saying he had information that led him to believe that two Mexicans and two Indians may have been involved in the abduction of the Marvin boy and were hiding him in that city. Donaghy had already alerted the department, and he had a special squad formed to begin a systematic search.

The information came from Joseph Pinebird, an Indian who lived in the neighborhood of Tenth and Pine Streets. He happened to talk with two Mexicans and two other Indians who had a young boy with them matching the description of Horace Marvin. Pinebird said they told him they had been paid by a white man at a place below Chester, Pennsylvania, to take charge of the boy.

Pinebird knew the four men well, having met them when he was employed in a Wild West show. He believed the Indians to be very quiet, but the Mexicans had a bad reputation. When they met on the street, the four men questioned Pinebird about where he lived, showing up at his place the following night with the boy. They told him that if he would take care of the boy at his house for a week, they would make it worth his time to do so. Pinebird declined and reported the encounter to Captain Donaghy. Of course, nothing came of the sighting, except the probable disruption of several Philadelphia households by the special police squad.[71]

Until this point, the attempts to locate Horace Marvin Jr. had been driven by ransom letters, the few local clues possibly left by the kidnappers or the sighting of the boy, all of which eventually proved to be useless. Two weeks into the disappearance, there was still no actual evidence the child was even alive.

There also appeared to be a breach of confidence between Dr. Marvin and the Pinkertons. Marvin believed the detectives had failed to adequately search for the child and were wasting time chasing down clues that never produced good leads. Superintendent Dimaio, for his part, believed that Marvin wasn't being totally open about what he knew about the disappearance or information he had privately obtained.

On Monday, March 18, Dr. Marvin, and his son Harry were out of town. When they finally arrived back at the Capitol Hotel, they were informed that the doctor had received several long-distance telephone calls during the day. The caller refused to leave a name and would not talk to the detectives or anyone else, stating that they would only talk to the doctor.

About 7:30 p.m., another long-distance call came in, and the doctor was called to the phone. A man on the other end asked if Marvin would like to talk to his son, to which the doctor answered, "Yes." A moment later, Dr.

Capitol Hotel, Dover, Delaware, circa 1907. *Delaware Public Archives.*

Marvin heard a faint voice that said, "Papa." The voice said a few more words, which were unintelligible for a while. The doctor then asked the child, "Do you know Harry?" to which the boy answered, "Yes." Marvin, now in tears, reportedly asked the voice on the phone other questions, to which the childlike voice replied. The call was then disconnected from the caller's end. The manager of the Bell Telephone Company exchange was later contacted and confirmed several long-distance calls had been put through to Dr. Marvin, but he had no way to know who had placed the calls, only that they came from Erie, Pennsylvania.

Later that evening, Dr. Marvin spoke to a reporter from the *New York Evening World* who had learned of the development. Marvin described the phone conversation and stated that unless this was a joke, he believed that little Horace would be back with him very soon.[72] The next day, Tuesday, March 19, readers of the *New York Evening World* woke to the headline:

KIDNAPPED BOY FOUND BY POLICE
Announce on Unquestioned Authority
That He Is Located in That
Vicinity and Will Be in Their
Custody in a Few Hours.

However, in keeping with the confused communications surrounding the case, the Kingston, New York *Daily Freeman* reported the same morning:

MARVIN MYSTERY MORE MUDDLED
Child's Voice Heard Over the Telephone
It Might Have Been the Missing Boy
Police at Erie Are in Absolute Ignorance[73]

The next day, the *New York Evening World* managed to contact the Erie chief of police, Edward Wagner. Wagner said he had gotten the story from Dover the previous evening that the child was in Erie. He then spoke with Chief Detzel of the Erie detectives, who were then searching for the boy. The only possible lead uncovered by the police was a report that an unidentified child was found alone on State Street in Erie, in front of a physician's home.

Chief Wagner told the reporter that on Monday afternoon a man came into his office and asked for copies of the police circular with a photo and information about the kidnapping. He gave them to him, and the man left without further conversation. Wagner described him as strange and heavyset, with a smooth face and black hair.

When questioned on his thoughts about the Erie lead, Dr. Marvin said that he had been disappointed so often he didn't know what to say. He had been urged to limit comments and guard his language to the newspapers, "although I recall that the press of the country is doing more for me than any other agency."[74]

Superintendent Dimaio had left Dover on Sunday night, returning Monday night after the telephone call with Erie. He sent two of his operatives to find Dr. Marvin, who was under doctor's orders to rest at the hotel after a near collapse following the call. Marvin went with the men and had what was described as a "vigorous" conversation in Dimaio's room. The conversation was so loud it could be heard in the halls of the hotel and again seemed to center on Dimaio's belief that Marvin wasn't turning all his mail over to the Pinkertons as he had agreed.

Later that night, after Dr. Marvin finally got to bed, another long-distance call was received from the Erie authorities. Speaking with Harvey Marvin, they reported that they believed they had located the boy. No one would reveal any of the conversation, but the reporters learned that the boy had been followed from Canada to Port Huron, Michigan, and then on to Erie: "The search now in progress is very complicated. Apparently no two persons are working in conjunction, and as a result numerous reports concerning the kidnapped lad are in circulation."[75]

On Tuesday morning, it was learned that the person who spoke with Dr. Marvin the previous evening was an Erie attorney, A.P. Howard. The general opinion was that Howard was not the kidnapper but had communication with them. They wanted to surrender the boy and obtain the ransom and expected Howard to arrange the exchange.

The identification of attorney Howard and the reported presence of the child in Erie immediately set off a race between the Erie police and the Pinkerton agents to locate the boy. Several Erie detectives said they had found a clue and, apparently without telling anyone else in their department, set out in several carriages to a location some miles outside the city. Five Pinkerton detectives discovered Howard had an office at 702 State Street, where, they assumed, he was also keeping the child. They searched from cellar to attic, without authority and without results. As for Howard himself,

Chief Wagner and several Pinkertons found him in his office and spent an hour and a half trying to learn the location of the child, to no avail.

Howard had admitted he was the one who contacted Dr. Marvin the previous evening, even pretending to be his son. But the lawyer wasn't as forthcoming about his call to the doctor on Tuesday. In that call, Howard offered to return the doctor's son if the father would sign an indemnity bond to safeguard the kidnappers from prosecution and escape the death penalty prescribed by Delaware law. However, Marvin and the Pinkertons wanted some conclusive proof to be given before agreeing to anything. All in Dover seemed to agree that the kidnappers had taken the boy before becoming acquainted with the Delaware law and now just wanted to avoid being hanged in the city jail yard.

Howard said a prominent physician in Erie had been approached by two women who said they had found a child on the street who looked like the missing Marvin child in the newspaper accounts. The women would not reveal their identities but would agree to turn the child over to his father if he would agree not to prosecute the kidnappers. The unnamed doctor declined to help but did refer the women to Howard, who immediately contacted Dr. Marvin.

Superintendent Dimaio had advised Marvin not to make any public comment about the Howard discussion until it was determined if such a deal was even lawful. State officials and legal experts had looked at the proposal and now believed that attorney Howard was making himself an accessory after the fact. The state statutes on kidnapping were carefully read, and it was clearly stated that any persons, lawyer or otherwise, who entered into an agreement before or after a kidnapping was liable to punishment. Howard was asking for a bond of $2,000 stipulating that the kidnappers would be immune from prosecution when the boy was returned.

Back in Erie, the authorities were tired of Howard's stalling tactics. And to make matters worse, after Howard's name became publicly connected in the kidnapping, a crowd gathered at his office and threatened him with lynching if he didn't give up the location of the child. On Wednesday, Erie mayor Michael Liebel Jr. and Erie County district attorney W. Pitt Gifford went to Howard's office and directed him to turn over the Marvin boy or face a Delaware charge of accessory after the fact of kidnapping. Howard agreed to surrender the child.

A conference was arranged, and shortly after midnight, the mayor, district attorney and assistant district attorney, the chief of police and several detectives from various private agencies accompanied Howard to a boardinghouse owned by Bell Stirks at 2124 Myrtle Street in Erie. Mrs. Stirks was apprised of the reason for their late-night visit and said she had two guests staying in her home, a Mrs. Norvelle and her young son, John, who were soon awake and with the visitors. Mrs. Norvelle explained that she and her son formerly lived in Fredonia, New York, and they were staying in Erie while awaiting the formalization of a divorce from her husband. The resemblance of her son to the description of Horace Marvin was so close that Chief of Police Wagner immediately placed everyone in the house under arrest. It wasn't until Dr. Bell, an Erie physician, could be called and came to the house that the mystery was resolved. Dr. Bell identified the boy as having been a patient of his before March 4, the day of Horace Marvin's disappearance.[76]

In Dover, the initial announcement of the imminent recovery of Horace produced extreme joy among those who heard it, especially for Dr. Marvin. Unfortunately, when the facts of the discovery arrived soon after, the doctor was again plunged into the deep despair that had been his companion for the past three weeks.

7
ADVERTISING A KIDNAPPING

Of course, this was not my boy. The great trouble with the people of the country who are finding boys, in a splendid effort to aid me, is that they look for a big boy instead of a baby. Horace was but three and a half years old and not a large baby at that. Simply look for a little, retiring light-headed baby.[77]

D
r. Marvin's exasperation following the Erie, Pennsylvania report came just a few weeks into an investigation that had thus far wasted time and resources on false sightings and poor leads. One cause of the problem was the publicity in the newspapers concerning the disappearance. Wide publicity for a missing child could cut both ways. More people looking for Horace could help locate him, but it also created more false sightings, and that was the primary result so far in this case.

From the descriptions and illustrations found in multiple newspapers, a reader would have little information to distinguish one white, four-year-old, blond, blue-eyed child from another. And as was shown in the Erie sighting, there were children who were so close to the description that it required additional information to prove it was not actually Horace. This would happen more than once during the search.

Furthermore, the extensive publicity contributed to the confusion in another manner. Despite the Marvin family having Miles Standish, who was experienced in working with advertising, there was no coordinated description presented to the press about how Horace was dressed, his personal appearance or the accuracy of images printed in the newspapers. And since most of the newspapers in the country relied on the material sent on the press newswires, and this information was often edited due to space limitations, the details became less accurate over repetition.

A review of newspaper accounts of the story illustrates the variety and accuracy of the information presented in the press, posters and postcards, as compared to the actual information reported by the family. This is not meant to be a thorough study of the newspaper accounts, or their effect on finding the child, but rather an example of a contributing factor in the difficulty to locate Horace.

The first news of Horace Marvin's disappearance was on the front page of the March 5, 1907 edition of the Wilmington, Delaware *News Journal*. That the disappearance was assumed to be the work of kidnappers was evident in the headline. "Baby in the Hands of Child Stealers," and the text, which described the searches being conducted and the fact that kidnappers were subject to the death penalty in Delaware.[78]

The next day, the *News Journal* ran a second article about the disappearance. This one, headlined "Abductors Yet Hold Little Horace Marvin," ran from page one to page two and included details of what was known or believed so far, running to what was almost a full column length of the paper. It included no details about the appearance of the victim.[79] Two additional short articles appeared over the next two days, still without a narrative, photograph or sketch of little Horace.

The *News Journal* finally published a description of Horace Marvin Jr. on page one of the March 9, 1907 edition, five days after his disappearance. Appearing at the top of the page under the headline "Believe They Have Spotted Kidnappers," the paper printed the description in a black-bordered box.[80]

The earliest article including a description and image of the boy appeared the same day in a prominent area of page one of the *Washington (D.C.) Times*. There was a photo of the child, wearing his Buster Brown suit, along with three sketches illustrating scenes connected with the disappearance and one sketch of Frank Butler. He was one of the men in the farmyard the morning Horace disappeared and believed by some to have had some involvement in the disappearance. The article also contained an information box with details on Horace's appearance that repeated the content of the *Evening Journal* article. Due to the limitations of reproduction techniques, newspaper photographs were often too dark or too light, and when the image was of a missing child, that could make the photograph difficult for identification.

The March 13, 1907 issue of the *Guthrie (OK) Daily Leader* had an eye-catching headline mentioning a $22,000 reward, but so far only the State of

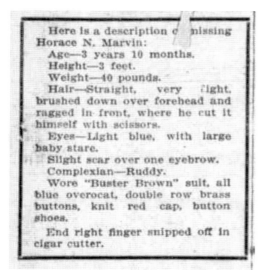

Here is a description of missing Horace N. Marvin:

Age—3 years 10 months.
Height—3 feet.
Weight—40 pounds.
Hair—Straight, very light, brushed down over forehead and ragged in front, where he cut it himself with scissors.
Eyes—Light blue, with large baby stare.
Slight scar over one eyebrow.
Complexion—Ruddy.
Wore "Buster Brown" suit, all blue overcoat, double row brass buttons, knit red cap, button shoes.
End right finger snipped off in cigar cutter.

Left: The first newspaper description of the missing child. *From the* Wilmington Evening Journal.

Opposite: Illustration for a newspaper article about the disappearance. *"Stolen Boy and Scenes near Home,"* Washington (D.C.) Times.

Delaware had offered a reward, and that was only $2,000. While Dr. Marvin had mentioned offering a reward, no amount had yet been stated.

The *Daily Leader* article does include a drawing of what is represented as Horace Marvin without his overcoat, wearing the Buster Brown outfit. In the text of the article, the reader is asked to "LOOK CLOSELY AT THIS LITTLE BOY'S FACE. HAVE YOU SEEN HIM ANYWHERE DURING THE PAST FEW DAYS?" Unfortunately for those looking for Horace, this generic drawing of a child was useless. The paper used a decorative box to highlight the boy's description but gave vague details, such as a "chubby" face and "large for his age," and the clothing description was so generic as to be of little use.

It's not known who placed the information on the newswire report that was seen by the *Daily Leader*, but there was one feature of the child that should have been included in every description. When Dr. Marvin had first visited Delaware in search of a farm, he brought his two young boys with him. While staying at the Capitol Hotel, young Horace had accidentally clipped off the tip of his right-hand little finger in a cigar cutter. Fortunately, the injury had healed, but it did leave an easily identifiable point of identification. Of the numerous descriptions that were printed in papers across the country, this fact was found only in the first descriptive reports in the March 9 *Evening Journal* and *Washington Times* articles and a poster prepared by Dr. Marvin and Miles Standish that is described on pages 74 and 75.

But the most likely cause of an incorrect identification by the public was the Buster Brown suit. The Buster Brown style of clothing was based on

Marvin Boy in Philadelphia, Colored Woman's Prisoner, Police Theory on Kidnaping

STOLEN BOY AND SCENES NEAR HOME

HOME OF DR. MARVIN

FRANK H. BUTLER

ROGERS

SHACK FROM WHICH BOY WAS TAKEN.

BROKEN RAIL OVER DITCH.

THE MISSING BOY

Age—Three years ten months.

Height—Three feet.

Weight—Forty pounds.

Hair—Straight, very light, brushed down over forehead, and ragged in front, where he cut it himself with a scissors.

Eyes—Light blue and large; a baby stare.

Slight scar over one eyebrow.

Complexion—Ruddy.

Buster Brown suit over his blue overalls. Blue overcoat, double row brass buttons. Knit red cap; button shoes.

End right finger snipped off in cigar cutter.

KEEP YOUR EYES OPEN FOR THIS KIDNAPPED BOY REWARD IS $22,000

○ ○ ○ ○ ○ ○ ○ ○ ○ ○ ○ ○ ○ ○ ○ ○
DESCRIPTION OF
    HORACE MARVIN, JR.

Horace Marvin, Jr.
Age—four years.
Size—large for his age.
Skin—light.
Hair—light.
Eyes—blue.
Face—chubby.
Dressed—Cap, knitted worsted toboggan with tassel; coat, dark blue, buttoning on one side only; baby overalls and jumper.

LOOK CLOSELY AT THIS LITTLE BOY'S FACE. HAVE YOU SEEN HIM ANYWHERE DURING THE PAST FEW DAYS? HE IS HORACE MARVIN, THE 4-YEAR-OLD SON OF DR. MARVIN, AND HE WAS KIDNAPPED ON MARCH 4 FROM HIS FATHER'S FARM IN DELAWARE. KEEP YOUR EYES OPEN FOR A CHILD LOOKING LIKE THE ABOVE. THERE IS A REWARD OF $22,000 OFFERED TO ANYONE WHO FINDS HIM. HE MAY BE IN ANY SECTION OF THE COUNTRY.

Illustration for a newspaper article about the disappearance. *From the* Guthrie (OK) Daily Leader.

that worn by a 1902 comic strip character of the same name. It consisted of a hip-length or longer double-breasted jacket, belted at the waist, worn with knee-length trousers and shirts with wide detachable collars. A large-brimmed straw hat worn over a pageboy-style haircut and boots or strapped shoes completed the style.[81] Regrettably, this was the most popular style of

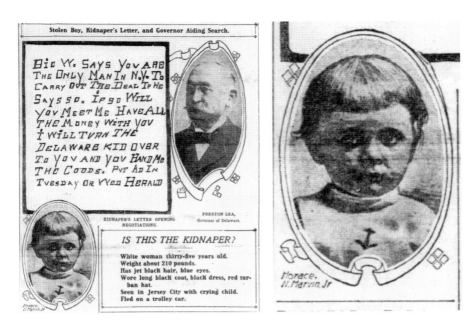

Left: Confusing group of images in an article about the missing boy. *From the* Washington (D.C.) Times.

Right: Photo detail showing the poor quality of most newspaper images of the missing boy. *From the* Washington (D.C.) Times.

children's clothing in 1907, and the first thing a person would notice when seeing a child in a public place.[82]

The same day the *Daily Leader* published its article, the *Washington (D.C.) Times* ran a confusing article that included a copy of a supposed kidnapper's ransom note, a photo of Delaware governor Lea and a description of a possible sighting of the child with a woman kidnapper in Jersey City, New Jersey. A small insert of a photographic image of Horace was dark, and the paper didn't take the opportunity to reprint the description.

Help in identifying Horace to the public wasn't just coming from newspapers. On March 10, Miles Standish and Dr. Marvin prepared a reward poster, reportedly the size of a newspaper sheet, printed on what was described as "fine plate paper." The photographic quality is probably the best of any of the images of young Horace that were published. Thousands of copies of the poster were produced and shipped from Dover to locations across the country.[83] The poster was also included in a *Harper's Weekly* article in its April 6, 1907 issue, which added visibility to the search. The poster is shown on the following page.[84]

KIDNAPPED!

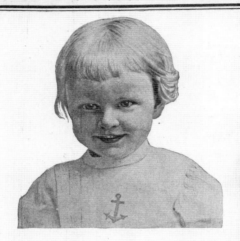

HORACE N. MARVIN, Jr.

This picture was taken sixteen months ago at the age of two years and six months.

A liberal reward will be paid for any information that will prove valuable in locating, rescuing or returning my four-year old child, stolen from his home, "Bay Meadows," seven miles east from Dover, Delaware, Monday morning, March 4th, 1907, at ten o'clock.

HEIGHT—Three feet.

WEIGHT—Forty pounds.

AGE—Three years and ten months on the day stolen.

HAIR—Very fair, light in growth, straight, brushed straight down over forehead. Ragged in front where he had cut it himself with scissors.

EYES—Light blue, large and wide open as in baby stare. This feature prominent. Slight scar on one eyebrow. Perceptible but not prominent.

TEETH—Regular, small, short and very white.

FACE—Round and complexion ruddy.

CLOTHING—Wears four-year-old size Buster Brown woolen suit, brown in color. Over this a pair of blue overalls and over all a blue overcoat with double row of large brass buttons. Knit cap, red, with Roman band and tassel of many colors. Leather, buttoned shoes.

While at hotel in Dover cut end first finger of right hand in cigar cutter. Cut has healed, but nail is cut square off. To trim it would necessitate cutting into the quick.

H. N. MARVIN, M. D.
Dover, Delaware.

Poster prepared and mailed across the country by Dr. Marvin. *Harper's Weekly.*

KIDNAPPED!
HORACE N. MARVIN, Jr.
This picture was taken sixteen months ago at the age of two years and six months.

A liberal reward will be paid for any information that will prove valuable in locating, rescuing or returning my four-year old child, stolen from his home, "Bay Meadows," seven miles east from Dover, Delaware, Monday morning, March 4ᵗʰ, 1907, at 10 o'clock.

Height—Three feet.
Weight—Forty pounds.
Age—Three years and ten months on the day stolen
Hair—Very fair, light in growth, brushed straight down over forehead. Ragged in front where he had cut it himself with scissors.
Eyes—Light blue and large and wide open as in baby stare. This feature prominent. Slight scar on one eyebrpw. Perceptible but not prominent.
Teeth—Regular, small, short, and very white.
Face—Round and complexion ruddy.
Clothing: Wears four-year-old size Buster Brown woolen suit. Brown in color. Over this a pair of blue coveralls and over all a blue overcoat with double row of large brass buttons. Knit cap, red, with Roman band and tassel of many colors. Leather, buttoned shoes.

While at hotel in Dover cut end of first finger of right hand in cigar cutter. Cut has healed, but nail is cut square off. To trim it would necessitate cutting into the quick.

H.N. MARVIN, M.D.
Dover, Delaware

Descriptive Poster sent throughout the
Country for Identification Purposes

$1,000 Reward

will be paid for the delivery of HORACE N. MARVIN, JR., to the undersigned. In making this offer I wish to make it very clear that the person delivering this lost boy to me will take no risk of arrest, but on the contrary, they can feel perfectly safe and know that I will not betray them and will arrange in a manner whereby escape from arrest or detection in any way will be certain.

I sacredly promise any one delivering this boy to me, that my lips shall be sealed and silent forever and I will never give the slightest clue that might lead to their arrest.

I will pay the cash without asking any questions whatever.

Sincerely,

Philadelphia, Pa. WILLIAM SPENCER, 2149 Germantown Ave

DESCRIPTION

Height, 3 feet; Weight, 40 pounds; Age, 3 years and 10 months Hair, very fair, brushed straight down over forehead, light in growth; Eyes, light blue, large and wide open as in baby stare—this feature prominent; slight scar on one eye brow—not prominent; Face, round; Complexion, ruddy.

These cards will be furnished free by SPENCER PRINTING CO., 2147 GERMANTOWN AVE. PHILA PA.

HORACE N. MARVIN, JR.
who disappeared from his father's farm near Dover, Del., on Monday morning, March 4, 1907.

MARVIN REWARD POST CARD,
Issued by William Spencer, of Philadelphia, and Obtainable From The Sunday Times.

The Spencer $1,000 reward postcard. *Library of Congress.*

There was one other privately funded campaign to attempt to get Horace Marvin safely returned to his family. It consisted of the Marvin Reward Postcard, produced in early April 1907 and initially distributed by William Spencer of Philadelphia, Pennsylvania. The card included a good photographic image of Horace, along with an abbreviated description. However, the stated purpose of Spencer's postcard was to encourage the kidnappers to surrender Horace to him, and Spencer would then pay the reward money and allow the kidnappers to go free. While the Reward Postcard did not result in Horace being returned to Spencer, it was responsible for bringing a diverse group of persons together in the search. The story is told in detail in chapter 9.

The previous examples were designed specifically to draw a reader's attention to the missing Marvin boy and provide information to aid in his recovery. However, many other newspapers simply added a drawing or photograph of Horace, apparently as an afterthought, without considering the quality of the image or the usefulness to the reader. The following images all appeared in newspapers across the United States and are presented as examples of what the public had to guide them in the Marvin search.

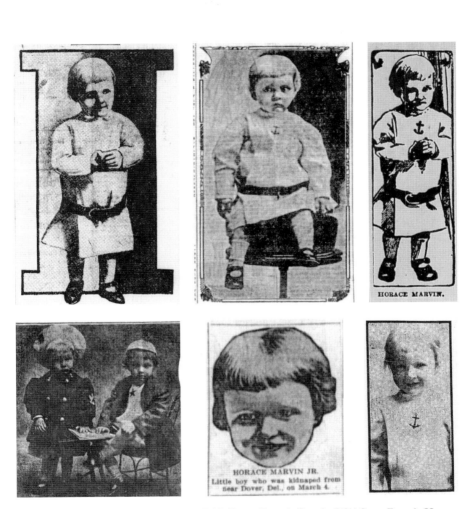

Clockwise from top, left: From the Spokane (WA) Press. *From the* Seattle (WA) Star. *From the* Hot Springs (SD) Weekly Star. *From the* Appeal (Saint Paul, MN). *From the* Seattle Star. *From the* Evening Journal (Wilmington, DE).

Clockwise from top, left: From the Evening Journal (Wilmington, DE). *From the* Albuquerque Evening Citizen. *From the* Fargo (ND) Forum and Daily Republican. *From the* Hawaiian Star. *From the* San Francisco Call.

8

THE BLACK HAND

The Erie case was closed, but there was always some other sighting or local clue to follow. On March 19, several Pinkerton detectives were sent to Bowers Beach to search any vacant houses. It was believed by reporters that the detectives thought the kidnappers might attempt to hide the boy near Bay Meadows and return him some night after dark, but nothing was found.

State detective Hawkins still had a few open leads, one being a well-known hermit named William Henze living near Cedar Beach, seven miles east of Milford, Delaware, on the Delaware Bay. Henze was reported to be about fifty-five years old and lived alone for the past six years in a combination cave/house he had built. His neighbors knew little about him other than every few months he would take a trip to New York. He was also assumed to have money, as he was never known to work.

Hawkins obtained a search warrant and checked the home in mid-March. Henze was not home but had left a note for any visitors saying he had left on March 13 to go to Bowers Beach. No one had seen him since. Hawkins looked around the place, but he found no connections with the Marvin case.[85]

Hawkins and his men then followed up a report of a Gypsy camp near Magnolia, about six miles south of Dover, where he found fifteen adults

Encampment of a group of Roma people. *Wikimedia Commons.*

and eight children. The word *Gypsy* is a pejorative term generally given to any band of itinerant people, but historically referred to the Roma, a separate ethnic group who originated in northern India around the eleventh century. As outsiders to the community, the Roma were often looked at as criminals and suspects in any crime that may have been committed in a town. Hawkins forced the members of the group to stand in line while they were given what was described as a "thorough examination," which included testing the skin of several children to see if it had been stained or dyed. Horace Marvin was not in the group.

The Pinkertons also had another sighting by two women in Upland, near Chester, Pennsylvania. A man dressed as a fisherman was seen dragging a small boy with light hair, wearing a Buster Brown suit and a coat with brass buttons, into the back of Bowery Row. The man reportedly cursed at the child while pulling him in a rough manner. The house they had been seen to enter was searched the next day, but nothing was found. Oddly enough, H.W. Bearce, the Pinkerton detective superintendent of the Philadelphia office, was quoted as saying this clue was considered to be the most plausible they had yet obtained.[86]

During this time, several Secret Service men were seen in Dover, leading to speculation they were there under orders of President Roosevelt to help in the Marvin disappearance. The agents volunteered only that they were there on a different matter.[87]

The visit of federal agents was coincidental with the Delaware Assembly preparing a resolution to be sent to President Roosevelt requesting his assistance with getting post offices to place posters alerting the public to the Marvin disappearance. Dr. Marvin contributed his own plea to the president with a personal telegram:

Your Excellency: As a sorrowing father of a missing child, I make bold to ask if government aid can be extended along two lines. Many threatening letters are sent to me every day saying my boy may be killed by his supposed captors, and it causes me much expense investigating these. They should be looked into.

I have sent out pictures and notices regarding my kidnapped baby boy, and I am told the postmasters are not allowed to display them in the public buildings. The Delaware legislature has voted two thousand dollars for the search for the boy, and has aided me in every possible way, but I believe a word from you to the federal authorities may be the greatest aid of all.

H.N. Marvin, Dover, Del.

The following day, Dr. Marvin received the President's reply:

My Dear Mr. Marvin,
I am in receipt of your telegram of the 22d instant. Anything that the government can do to help you will of course be done, for save only the crime of assault upon women there is none so dreadful as that which has brought heart-breaking sorrow to your household. I have at once communicated with the Post Office Department asking that all aid we have in our power to give along the lines you mention, or in any other that may prove practicable, be given to you.
Sincerely yours, Theodore Roosevelt

The next day, it was learned that a general order was issued under the direction of Postmaster General George Meyer, at the insistence of the president, that the writers of letters to Dr. Marvin were to be watched. The letters would be carefully examined, and any of a criminal nature would be investigated. However, the postmaster general could not permit the display of posters, pictures or descriptions of the missing boy, as it was against federal regulations, not a Post Office Department directive.[88]

Three weeks into the disappearance of Horace, the Pinkerton agents at Bay Meadows were now twenty strong and had not found a single clue that the boy had been kidnapped. However, at Dr. Marvin's urging, they did another search of the property.

The usual number of sightings continued to arrive. The latest were in Buffalo, New York, and Toronto, Canada; however, Pinkerton agents in those cities were not aware of the information. There was also the first of what would be several sightings outside of North America.

On March 19, a pharmacist named Phillips was in Portsmouth Harbor on the south coast of England. Phillips was waiting for a boat to take him to his home across the harbor when his attention was directed to two men with a small boy, who repeatedly asked, "When are you going to take me to my father?" Phillips found the repetition peculiar, and the next day when he saw a newspaper account of the Marvin kidnapping, he recognized the description of the boy as the same one he had seen on the dock and contacted police.

Given the various transportation options available to a traveler in 1907, it would have been possible for someone to leave Dover, Delaware; take a train to New York; and book passage on an ocean liner, all in the same day. A trip to England would normally have taken a week to ten days. But regardless of their destination, the traveler, and any children, would have needed some degree of paperwork: identification, passports, visas and the like, all of which had to be obtained before boarding a ship. Anyone planning to abduct a child to take out of the country would have to either have proper documents prepared beforehand or be able to hide the child long enough for papers to be obtained. As in any era, false documents were available but risky if you were kidnapping someone. So, getting Horace Marvin from Kitts Hummock to Portsmouth, England, in fifteen days would have theoretically been possible but probably exceedingly difficult in practice. However, the sighting by Phillips had to be treated as legitimate.

Because of the American connection, when the Portsmouth police received Phillips's information, they contacted John Main, the American consul-general, who immediately contacted a Mr. Swalm, the American counsel at Southampton. Swalm quickly found that the boy had arrived at Southampton on March 19 on the Atlantic Transport Line steamer *Minneapolis*, which had left New York on March 10. The boy did not take the train to London with the other passengers, and it was assumed he probably went to Portsmouth. Scotland Yard, local police and Pinkerton detectives were soon on the case. Within two days, the case was closed. The boy was found to be the child of English parents, and all were well known in Portsmouth.[89]

In 1907, the rural Kitts Hummock area had the traditional one-room schoolhouse typical of Delaware at the time. The Logan School, as it was called, was built sometime before 1866, as it shows up on maps of that period, and was located about two miles south of the Marvin farm.

Lucy Killen was the Logan School teacher in 1907 and, like almost all public school teachers of the time, an unmarried woman. She was the daughter of Dover policeman Thomas Killen and lived at a boardinghouse near the school. On Tuesday afternoon, March 19, Lucy left the school and walked her usual path home through the woods; at one point, she became aware of the voices of men near the path. One was saying, "They will never get the boy until we get…" Then the voice suddenly stopped, and a man stepped in front of her holding a revolver. He was quickly joined by a second man, also armed with a revolver.

The two men closely questioned Lucy: *Who was she… where did she live… what did she know about the recent events in the neighborhood?* They didn't harm her but did leave her with a warning that she would be killed if she told anyone of their meeting or what she might have heard.

When she reached the boardinghouse, she told the housekeeper, D.K. Moore, about the encounter. He immediately contacted neighbors and formed a search party, which soon grew to over one hundred men. The search continued all night, watching the roads and farm lanes leading out of the area.

Three respected local men believed they had seen the two strangers around the time they accosted Killen. Gilbert Marvel and Harry Knotts saw them from a distance at a crossroads about two miles from the Marvin farm. The third man, Henry Wright, a commissioner of the Logan School, met the strangers rapidly driving their carriage away from the Kitts Hummock area toward Magnolia. Both were wearing blue suits and dark brown fedora hats, a style not worn locally. No traces of the men were ever found.

The next morning, Killen gave a signed statement, and detectives planned to have her look at several men who had been under suspicion in the Marvin disappearance. This included Frank Butler, who had been on Bay Meadows farm the morning of the disappearance. However, she did not recognize any of the men.[90]

Nothing developed from the investigation of Killen's experience. The Pinkertons continued to watch the roads but maintained their skepticism about the entire kidnapping. Even with the three eyewitnesses to strangers in the area, the public was doubtful of the meeting. Her father, on the other hand, was considering having her withdraw from the school for her safety.

On March 29, ten days after the encounter in the woods, Killen and two of her students arrived at the school to find a note pinned to the door.

"BEWARE—YOU TOLD." In one corner of the note was a crudely made symbol of a skull and crossed bones. Inside the school, Killer found the room had been ransacked and something burned in the stove.

> *All the ashes had been raked out of the stove and scattered all over the place. The clock was thrown down and my calendars were torn, and the outer vestibule door was left open. I was not half so frightened when those men stopped me in the woods, and then allowed me to go, as when I saw that schoolroom, and I broke down entirely. I have not been able to eat or sleep....*
>
> *I saw at a glance that somebody had broken into the schoolhouse. They had pried open a window shutter and had raised a window which had been held down by a long nail....* [91]

The note renewed her friends' confidence in the threat from the men in the woods, as well as the belief that there was a Black Hand gang working near Bay Meadows. The idea was reinforced by the location of the encounter with Killen. That area was well hidden from view of the main roads and was crisscrossed by internal roads and farm lanes; it could have provided access to an abandoned farmhouse to possibly hide a kidnapped boy. It was expected that the kidnappers would approach Dr. Marvin on one of his many solitary trips back and forth to Dover to negotiate the return of his son. However, Marvin continued his trips uninterrupted, the men searching Kent County for the headquarters of the Black Hand found nothing and the fate of Horace Marvin Jr. remained unknown.

While the eyes of the detectives and the press were focused on a nonexistent Kent County Black Hand, a potentially more ominous situation was occurring near Atlantic City, New Jersey. Around five o'clock on Thursday afternoon, March 20, two Black women got off a trolley car at North Somers Point, about five miles inland from Atlantic City. Between them was a small white boy, whose appearance was reported by several people to appear in "a general way" to resemble the newspaper images of Horace Marvin Jr. The trio then disappeared down a lonely road leading into the southern end of the Pine Barrens forest of South Jersey. The sighting was confirmed by the conductor of the trolley and by Jacob Schich, the owner of a local hotel, who drove by the trio in his carriage and remembered the boy had light hair and was crying. The information was passed to local officials, who called the Atlantic City police, while local men began a search an hour after dark.[92]

The following day, it was reported that the entire countryside was "aroused and in the hunt." A farmers' posse and detectives from Atlantic City began searches of any deserted buildings or wood chopper camps in the area. According to newspaper accounts, whether the women were the actual kidnappers of the boy or not, there was "some deep mystery connected with their suspicious action and mysterious disappearance." The "hunting parties," as they were described, returned to Somers Point late into the night, "the negro [*sic*] women eluding their pursuers in some manner in the deep woods" (emphasis added).

The search of a possible four-by-five-square-mile area in the immediate vicinity of the initial sighting was to be continued the following day, deep into the thick pine woods. Apparently, neither the women nor the boy was ever located.[93]

The end of March finally saw Dover detective Murphy contact his family by telephone from Philadelphia. Murphy proudly reported he had been in Mechanicsville, New York, where he had caused the arrest of a Black man walking in town with a little white boy, and two Italians.[94] The Italians were arrested on suspicion, apparently just for being Italian, as no particular charge was mentioned. The unfortunate Black man was soon released when it was shown that the boy was the son of a nearby farmer who had asked the man to bring the boy into town for a haircut.[95]

Governor Lea met with Pinkerton superintendents Bearce and Dimaio to discuss his authorizing their arrest of a suspect in the Marvin case. The Pinkertons had been closely watching two unidentified men and believed they had enough evidence against one man to justify an arrest. The governor declined the request, expressing his concern that, given the local feelings surrounding the case, any arrest might result in the death of an innocent man.[96] The Pinkertons were to keep the men under surveillance.

There was a moment of excitement when it was learned that someone had reported that Horace Marvin's body might have been buried in a cemetery outside of the town. Detectives investigated the sighting and learned that five nights previously, someone had been seen burying a body. The grave was found, located on a piece of private ground next to the cemetery. When the grave was opened, it was found to contain the remains of a Black infant.[97]

9

HERE, THERE AND NOWHERE

The second month of the Horace Marvin Jr. disappearance began about the same as the first one had ended. In Washington, D.C., that Monday morning, the telephone rang in the detective bureau of the Metropolitan Police Department. The officer who answered the call heard a woman's voice: "Little Horace Marvin is held a captive in a house not a hundred yards from the place I am talking from now. Send a detective here right away."[98]

Detectives were sent to the home in the Seaton Place NE section of the city. When they arrived, the lady directed them to a nearby two-story frame dwelling, located on a slight knoll. She said it was occupied by the family of an oyster dredger, and she was sure the young Marvin was there, as she had seen him in a vision. The detectives' check of the home found it occupied by a family with a young blond-haired boy, but it wasn't Horace.

The *Washington Times* published the news that Pinkerton agents would be searching for the missing child in the district, and the news likely increased false alarms of sightings. According to a policeman, "Everybody who has seen visions of the child in their sleep will be telephoning police headquarters."[99]

The first of April 1907 was four weeks into the investigation of Horace Marvin's disappearance, and there was still no reliable evidence of his whereabouts or even if he was dead or alive. Even the old barn on the Marvin farm was taken apart piece by piece but produced no new clues.

The detectives working the case were all in Dover for the day, having nothing new to pursue. Pinkerton detective superintendent Dimaio and several of his agents were going back to Philadelphia, leaving a few in Dover to cover anything that might arise. The general opinion was that this kidnapping had been planned, like that of Charlie Ross in Philadelphia in 1874.

The Ross kidnapping is considered the first kidnapping for ransom in the United States and occurred on July 1, 1874. Four-year-old Charley Ross was playing in his front yard with his five-year old brother, Walter, when a carriage stopped and the driver offered them candy and fireworks if they would go with him, which they did. When they stopped to buy the fireworks, the driver abandoned Walter and drove away with Charley still in the carriage. He was never seen again.

Dr. Marvin left the farm and moved to the Capitol Hotel to be able to handle the daily volume of telegrams and mail. Morning and afternoon mail deliveries were routine in Dover in 1907, and forty or more letters, packages and special deliveries were common. The supposed Black Hand letters were still coming in on occasion. Their demands kept getting lower and lower, reaching as little as two hundred dollars, hoping that Dr. Marvin would simply send money for the faint promise of the return of his son. But most of the correspondence came from honest people who just wanted to offer advice or moral support to the distraught father. Some sent prayers or even small amounts of money. Every parent could relate to the pain of his loss and wanted to see the child safely returned to his home.

Some letters came from people who wanted to help find his son, and others even believed they had him under surveillance. One particular writer, Mrs. J.J. Heiser of St. Albans, Long Island, was quite sure she knew exactly where Horace was and had taken the liberty to write to William Randolph Hearst, the publisher of the *New York Journal*. "So we shall know very soon whether we are mistaken or not," she wrote to Dr. Marvin. She told Hearst the boy was at the Hippodrome Theater, a building that took up an entire city block and seated 5,300 people.[100]

The only things pending in Dover were the usual sightings with vague descriptions and often racial or ethnic inference. A sighting in South

Norwalk, Connecticut, was typical. Harlan L. Phillips, the general agent for the Fleischmann Yeast Company, was on an express train one afternoon traveling from New York to Ridgefield, Connecticut. Phillips saw a young boy he believed was the missing Marvin child in the custody of three Italian men, who, according to Phillips, were keeping the boy quiet by "forcing him to drink some drug from a bottle." Phillips brought the situation to the attention of train conductors Charles Vaughn and Daniel McNulty, both of whom agreed the matter looked suspicious. While Phillips and the conductors were deciding what they should do, the train stopped at Branchville, and the three men and the boy got off and disappeared in the crowd.[101]

The Delaware legislature had publicly stated its intention to do whatever it took to solve this mystery, but the $2,000 it had appropriated was rapidly being depleted. Secretary of State Joseph Cahall was asked about this by reporters but avoided answering by saying it was the responsibility of the governor and attorney general. He did note that the governor had a contingency fund of $1,200 and the attorney general $1,400 that could be applied to the search.

Dr. Harvey Marvin, the half brother of young Horace, was preparing to return to South Dakota on personal business when he was interviewed by a reporter in Philadelphia. When asked if he thought his little brother was dead, he said,

> *No. I do not know why I say this, but I feel we shall see him alive again. I don't believe in giving up in an uneven fight like this until I have gone the limit. I must say however, that we have gone pretty near the limit. At times I am inclined to the belief that the little fellow's body is somewhere in the vicinity of the farm. I do not mean on our farm, because searching parties have covered every foot of it, but in the neighborhood. I think the key to the mystery is right down in or about Dover. There are folks down there who might in my estimation, tell a few things if they opened up.*[102]

In March, when Dr. Marvin had commented that "the press of the country is doing more for me than any other agency," he wasn't practicing flattery or sarcasm. The first reports of the disappearance were quickly put on the newswires and sent across the country and eventually around the world. Within weeks, there were over one thousand American newspaper articles on the subject in every state and most territories. Most of Europe was following the story, and it traveled westward to Hawaii,[103] Australia and even Whanganui, a small town on the North Island of New Zealand.[104]

It is hard not to read an American newspaper from the early twentieth century without finding short news items about a local murder, domestic violence or a deadly railroad accident, many of which involved children. These articles might be two or three column inches, present the details to the reader and then move on to the next item of the day. Some of these might have gotten on the newswire and picked up and placed in another community's newspaper, but usually their interest to the general reader was limited to the hometown audience. The Horace Marvin disappearance, as tragic as it was to the Marvin family, should have fit this mold. A four-year-old child disappears from a farm in a small community in rural Delaware that few people except the locals would even know existed, yet the story became international news in a matter of days.

Three days after Horace disappeared, the boy's uncle, Miles Standish, arrived in Dover. In better times, Standish and his wife, Rose, lived in New York City, where he worked in publishing and advertising for newspapers and magazines. Standish was a quiet, behind-the-scenes character in this drama. He wasn't the rugged western type, like the Marvin men, but he knew his way around a city, and that is what was needed. Dr. Marvin often sent him to check on reported sightings of Horace, especially when they were in the greater New York region. Standish knew the many small communities from North Jersey to southern Connecticut, and he could use the opportunity to stop and talk with his contacts among the newspaper and magazine publishers. It is also possible Standish was what would later be known as an anonymous source, giving information on the investigation directly to editors.

Miles Standish wasn't the only one actively supporting the search for Horace Marvin. In April, a Philadelphia resident and printer, William Spencer, was a parent who sympathized with Dr. Marvin. He also added another $1,000 to the reward money for Horace Marvin's return and promised immunity to the kidnappers. Spencer was probably not aware the State of Delaware had already eliminated that option.

Spencer also believed that his reward would prove an attractive option to the abductors, as they would be unwilling to return to Dover to deliver the boy. He, on the other hand, could offer a neutral area to receive the child and pay the ransom. "If there should come to me, from any quarter of the earth at any hour of the day or night an offer to negotiate, I would take it up, and if the negotiator balked at the price, I would deal with them for a greater sum."[105]

While Spencer's understanding of Delaware law was flawed, he did add a new strategy to get visibility for the missing child—postcards. He had several thousand cards printed and mailed to individuals or sent in bulk at no charge to those who asked for them.

The *Washington (D.C.) Sunday Times* took the social involvement with the Marvin disappearance to another level. The paper had closely covered the case from the beginning and developed a significant following among its readers, many of whom sent letters and opinions—and even advice for Dr. Marvin—to the paper daily. On April 7, the paper asked the readers to think about the questions everyone was asking, including the authorities.

> *"What Is Your Answer?"*[106]
> *After reading all that has been made public in regard to this most mysterious of all recent kidnapping cases, the question still remains unanswered, "Was Horace Marvin stolen, or did he drown in the marsh of Bay Meadows Farm?" If he was abducted. How did his captors get away with him so quickly and in which direction did they go? Is the boy now somewhere within a radius of a few miles from his home, or is he far away?*

Many of the writers gave their opinions of these questions, including schoolchildren. Others wrote of a family member of theirs who had been lost, even briefly, and how they felt during that time. One young girl suggested how to identify if a child was Horace by simply asking his name. Another child thought schoolchildren would like to help, maybe simply by sending a nickel or a dime to the newspaper as a fund to help locate the child.

The paper also contacted William Spencer in Philadelphia. He sent boxes of his **KIDNAPPED** postcards to the *Times*, which then offered them, free of charge, to any readers who wished to use them to expand the search for Horace Marvin.

The *Washington Times'* idea was picked up by other papers, and the following week, it announced that eight additional papers from New York, Nebraska, Minnesota, Iowa and Missouri had started a similar "What Is Your Answer?" feature.

The wide interest in the Marvin case, as evidenced by the public interest in the stories in the *Washington Times*, spawned even greater curiosity in not only what had happened to the child but also how the mystery could be solved. In 1907, the adventures of Sir Arthur Conan Doyle's fictional sleuth Sherlock Holmes were almost as popular in America as in England, and one reporter for the *Milwaukee Journal* newspaper believed Holmes's methods could be successfully applied to solve the Marvin disappearance.

William H. Briggs went to Delaware as a detective, not a reporter. According to his account, Briggs spent a week in Dover, "making a complete and painstaking study of the case." Having walked over the farm, spoken to locals and collected all the available evidence, Briggs decided to apply the first rule of the Holmes method of crime deduction: "When you have eliminated the impossible, whatever remains, however improbable, must be the truth."[107]

Under the Holmes reasoning, Briggs immediately eliminated any possibility Horace Marvin was the victim of outright murder or suicide and determined there was almost no possibility he was the victim of immediate accidental death. No body had been found, nor was there evidence of a violent attack, which would have left signs of a struggle or cries from the boy if he were being forcibly carried away from the farmyard. Briggs concluded that, based on what had been determined thus far, Horace was alive.

The next considerations were if Horace became lost or, perhaps, ran away. Given the extensive searching of the Marvin farm and adjacent areas around Kitts Hummock without finding any trace of Horace, he was not lost. And given his age and size, it would not have been possible for him to get far from the farm before being seen by the searchers, who began looking for him within minutes of his last being seen.

Therefore, according to Briggs's interpretation of the Holmes method, the only possibility to consider was kidnapping. Since the Marvin family was new to Delaware, and had no known arguments with anyone, there was no motive for revenge against the family. However, it was generally believed that Dr. Marvin was a wealthy man, which could easily be a motive to obtain quick money. But given the Delaware law establishing death to kidnappers, nobody from Delaware was responsible, and Horace had to still be alive if kidnappers had any chance of getting money for his safe return. So, according to Briggs's logic, the kidnapper was someone who happened to be passing through Delaware, knew how to avoid detection, could travel light and obtain food and was the obvious person to have taken Horace…in other words, a hobo.

The word *hobo* is often thought of as a generic name for homeless drifters who traveled across the country on freight trains in the nineteenth and early twentieth centuries. As these transients were perceived as criminals, their presence in a community got the attention of police, who often moved them out of town to protect people and property. Hobos were seen in the same light as the Roma, Italians, Irish and almost anyone else who was outside the cultural norm of a neighborhood. In fact, most hobos were migrant laborers, using the railroads to travel for seasonal work or just job hunting during a depressed economy. While some were criminals, even Sherlock Holmes himself might question the logic of a traveler in a strange land deciding to kidnap a random child, find a place to hide them until a way could be found to contact the parents with a ransom demand and then collect the money and successfully escape the mob of people likely to be looking for them. But William H. Briggs did keep the story in the public mind and even got them thinking about how the crime may have occurred and how to solve it.

April 17 and 18 were days ranging from comedic relief to the dashing of hope. It began with a letter in the morning mail from the Black Hand in Hoboken, New Jersey. The writer said he had Horace in his custody, and if his father would place an advertisement in a certain New York newspaper with a location to meet, he would deliver the boy for $1 million. The back of the letter had the obligatory crude drawing of a black hand. Rather than think about what his options might be, Dr. Marvin simply sent the letter to the Hoboken police. The letter was signed Salvatore Antone. Apparently, Antone forgot he was writing an extortion letter.[108]

Dr. Marvin was expecting to be able to add New Jersey state detective Frank Lore to the Delaware payroll. New Jersey governor Stokes had approved his loan, and Governor Lea was to approve it. Lore told Marvin that he could find the child in a week. He had previously investigated a case on the Jersey shore that brought him into contact with the watermen. In a chance conversation with one of the fishermen, the subject of Horace Marvin had come up. "How much will you give me to tell you where that kid is?" the man inquired. Lore didn't follow up the question at the time, but he told Marvin that he believed the man did know something about the disappearance. Marvin hoped he was as good as his reputation.

And as far as reputations went, Kent County deputy constable Frederick Murphy was not living up to his. Since Dr. Marvin had taken him on as an independent detective a month ago, he had traveled a good bit but had communicated little to the doctor and visited Dover even less. The word around Dover was he had occasionally sent a postcard to his mother.

The mood turned more somber with the realization that most of the Pinkertons were leaving. A few were still checking on a couple of dead-end leads, but there was nothing for them to do in Dover, and they could be put on other agency cases.

Then, in late morning on the seventeenth, a man came to the hotel from the Marvin farm with the news that Horace's body had been located in the woods near the farm. The doctor left to go to the farm, weighed by the grief that his son was dead but rejoicing at finally having him back.

At the farm, Dr. Marvin was told there had been a mistake. A wake of buzzards had been seen, and someone said it was the boy, but when the area was examined, the birds were after an animal carcass. A farmer told a reporter that Dr. Martin looked so excited at the thought his child's body had been found and five years older when it had not.[109]

There was a slight flurry of excitement on April 18 when a child matching Horace's description was seen in a boat with two men on the lower Eastern Shore of Maryland near Cambridge. A sheriff's posse searched the area for the rest of the day and into the next before it was discovered the boat was just being used to help a family move to a new farm up the Wicomico River.[110]

Later that day, a melancholy message was received from Bergen Point, New Jersey. John Carson, the lighthouse keeper at the Kill van Kull waterway between New Jersey and New York, found a young boy's body on the rocks. It was reported to be about four years old and corresponded to the description. It was estimated to have been in the water about a month and needed to be identified as soon as possible.

To Dr. Marvin, who still held to the theory that Horace had been kidnapped and taken up the Delaware River to the North Jersey–New York City area, this could well be his child. He immediately took the afternoon train to Jersey City and, from there, rushed to the lighthouse. There he found the body tied to the rocks with ropes to keep it from being washed away by the tide.

Over the previous six weeks, Dr. Marvin had lived his life as if on a boat in a storm. It was never calm or quiet, always battered by forces beyond his control and threatening to drown him in the thought he would never see his son again, dead or alive.

The doctor steeled himself for the ordeal as he slowly worked his way over the rocks. He really believed the child was Horace. A reporter noted that "he dolefully shook his head as he looked at the body, turning aside and brushed the tears from his eyes." The body was later identified as that of an eight-year-old girl who had fallen into the waterway two weeks earlier.[111]

Back in Dover, the focus was on the new grand jury that was to begin its term on Monday, April 22. Since the Pinkertons had finished their investigations, there was speculation they would present their final bill for the work to the attorney general. The rumor was they also would have one or more prisoners and confessions or, at least, some incriminating admissions.

The Pinkerton Agency always had a policy of not providing public accounts of its investigations, but after watching the agents' movements for the past month, the public were of one of two opinions. The first was that the Pinkertons didn't have the faintest idea what had happened to Horace or where he was currently located. The second was that the detectives had figured out everything and would present the results of their work to the grand jury, but they still didn't know where the boy was.

Regardless of the work of the detectives, the grand jury had its own ideas about how it might proceed. There was believed to be a feeling among the jury members, and much of the public, that the investigators had not looked closely enough at the people who were on the farm the day Horace disappeared. There were still concerns that their explanations were being taken at face value. The grand jury could compel all the family members, as well as Woodall, Butler and Caldwell, to give testimony under oath about the exact events of that day. According to several grand jury members who had been interviewed by the *Wilmington Sunday Morning Star*, they were "unwilling to adjourn without doing anything or simply taking the word of the detectives that they are making all progress possible."[112]

Dr. Marvin had his own ideas on the work of the Pinkertons. He understood they took nothing for granted and were of the view that Horace was still on the farm. They had searched the grounds, buildings, ditches and wells within a two-mile radius of the house. When he was asked his opinion by a reporter, he said, "After working on the case for thirty days they have no clue."[113]

Local people or local people's employees must have done this thing, for no stranger could get off, particularly from the house to the bay. Thinking nobody was there, they came for plunder. Finding the house occupied, and the little one alone on the stack, on the impulse they took him for a reward. Later, learning the penalty, they did not dare to return him or to negotiate. Now, they have either sent him out of the country, or they have thrown my little boy into the bay to cover their crime.[114]

10

BUTLER DID IT

From the first days following the disappearance of his son, Dr. Marvin was focused on the Delaware Bay and River as the escape route used by kidnappers. The activities of the black-hulled sloops, the trail of Horace sightings from Chester to Philadelphia to Camden and New York City and even the supposed Canadian connection all seemed to point to north. Dr. Marvin routinely committed his investigative resources of the Pinkertons and his brother-in-law Miles Standish to these sightings. And he had given his ace Dover detective Frederick Murphy a free hand to follow any leads he developed, all of which seemed to be in the North Jersey and New York City region. Even though all the past leads proved false, the doctor was excited about one more sighting that seemed to finally be true.

In early March 1907, a man and a woman, with a young, fair-haired boy, were in Catskill, New York, staying at the West Shore Hotel under the name Alexander H. Allen. Allen was a peddler, or traveling salesman, representing a company in New York City that made gas mantles.

During the day, Allen went about town, selling his goods to local merchants and citizens, and took his meals at the hotel with his family, but he never slept there. Allen frequently left Catskill, taking his wife, but she would always leave the boy in the care of the hotel, with strict orders that the boy was not to leave the room. By all accounts, the boy seemed happy, telling people he had traveled many miles. Around the end of March, the Allens unsuccessfully tried to find someone to permanently take the boy, telling people they were going south. On March 28, all three left town, going to Gloversville, New York, about eighty miles northwest of Catskill. They also left an unpaid bill at the hotel.

In Gloversville, the Allens found rooms at a boardinghouse operated by a blind man, M.W. Lent. Their arrival attracted the attention of the police, who interviewed the man and woman. Allen told the police they were from New Haven, Connecticut, and he was a traveling salesman for a New York business. The police had no cause for action against the pair, but since the boy closely resembled the description of Horace Marvin, a watch was placed on the house. Several days later, a man was seen appearing to tiptoe from the house early in the morning. He was stopped and found to be Allen. He was then arrested on the suspicion of having not paid his hotel bill in Catskill and taken to police headquarters for questioning.

Under interrogation, Allen stood by his story, claiming he had been living in Catskill at the time of the Marvin kidnapping. He asked if he was being held on the Marvin matter. Upon being told yes, Allen reportedly dropped his head and said, "The expected, or rather the unexpected, has happened."[115]

The Gloversville police contacted Dr. Marvin by telephone and informed him of the situation. Marvin immediately sent a telegram to Miles Standish, who was in Boston, and told him to go to Gloversville to examine the Allen boy. Dr. Marvin soon received a photograph of the boy from the Gloversville police. After examining it, he quickly telegraphed Standish, "I think the boy is Horace." The doctor remained close to the telephone late into the night, believing this was one of the best leads yet received.

While awaiting the arrival of Miles Standish, the Gloversville police spoke with the boy, whose description reportedly closely fit that published in the newspapers, even down to the scar over his right eye. The boy said that his mother was dead, and his father called him "Chubby" and "Hello Pete." He also had a brother named Johnnie. However, the boy did not answer to the name Lowell, which, according to the couple he was traveling with, was his given name.

The police had managed to trace the travels of the Allens from Washington to Philadelphia and then to New York. The trio had then gone to Brooklyn before returning to New York, then up to Mechanicsville, where they spent a night at the home of a farmer.

When Dr. Marvin learned of their itinerary, it matched a lead he had received several weeks earlier from a man named Barber in Mechanicsville. Marvin sent Dover detective Frederick Murphy to investigate, where he spent several weeks traveling around Saratoga County, New York, searching for the boy. The trail had gone cold, but Murphy had remained in the area.

Learning of the Gloversville contact, Murphy traveled there and spoke with the two adults and the boy. He informed Dr. Marvin that, based on the information he had developed during his work in Saratoga County, he had no doubt the Gloversville police had the right man in custody. Now, with the Gloversville police reopening the Mechanicsville connection, Dr. Marvin was eager to have the opinion of Miles Standish.

Standish arrived in Gloversville early on April 21 and was immediately taken by the police chief to see the boy. Standish carefully examined the child and then spent half an hour playing with him. After more than an hour with the boy, Standish told the police chief that, while there was a resemblance to Horace, there were many points of difference. For example, the Allen boy's face was elongated, where Horace's was round. Horace had a scar over his right eye from a cut; the Allen boy's scar was from a burn. Both boys had noticeable differences in their hair color and the condition of their teeth, both points being clearly mentioned in some reward fliers. And finally, a detail not officially known, Horace was very ticklish, while the Allen boy was not.

Standish immediately wired Dr. Marvin: "Child held is not Horace. Convinced there are the parties Murphy trailed. Believe they know more than has been disclosed. Wire your convictions."[116]

Following the Standish examination, the boy and his mother were released from police custody, but the man was held for the outstanding warrant from the Catskill police. Dr. Marvin didn't commit any more time or resources to the Allens.

While the focus of the Marvin disappearance was directed toward Gloversville, the new session of the Kent County Grand Jury was meeting in Dover, and the jurors were anxious to move on the Marvin case. At their first session on Monday, April 22, they called New Jersey state detective Frank Lore.

Lore presented the findings of his investigation, which centered on the events on the morning of March 4 in the yard of Bay Meadows farm and the people who were present that morning. He believed that as Butler and Caldwell were leaving the barn with the loaded wagon, young Horace either climbed down or slid off the straw stack and was run over and killed by the wagon driven by Frank Butler. The grand jury voted for immediate action and issued a secret indictment for the abduction and possible murder of

No. 3551   Steamer John P. Wilson, Bowers, Del.

The steamer *John P. Wilson*, circa 1907. *Delaware Public Archives.*

Horace N. Marvin Jr. State Detective Hawkins then swore out the warrant for Butler's arrest in front of Justice of the Peace Edwin F. Wood.

On the day the warrant was issued, Butler was working as a deckhand on the Dover and Philadelphia Navigation Company's steamer *John P. Wilson*. The company carried general cargo and passengers, as well as summer excursion groups and persons making connections to other points. The Delaware attorney general and the detectives decided to arrest Butler while he was working on Wednesday night, April 24.

The *John P. Wilson* was scheduled to leave Philadelphia's Arch Street dock late in the evening, and detectives Hawkins and Lore and another New Jersey detective, Alonza Woodruff, booked staterooms for the trip. Before the boat left the dock, Hawkins showed Butler the warrant for his arrest. According to Hawkins, Butler expressed no emotion, only saying, "I'm glad this case is coming to an end."[117]

The evening was also marked by the return of the Pinkerton detectives. After the grand jury indictment was published, they returned to Dover, and before the *John P. Wilson* left, three men, including Superintendent Bearce, arrived at the dock. They surprised Hawkins and Lore by asking them not to serve the arrest warrant on Butler, which they refused to agree to. Just before the boat departed, one of the Pinkertons, Assistant Superintendent H.H. Lintner, went on board and paid for a stateroom. He was seen briefly speaking to Butler but made no attempt to prevent Butler's arrest, nor did he take any part in it.

It was speculated the reason the Pinkertons requested the Delaware detective not arrest Butler was it would then allow them to detain him, giving them the credit for the capture, as well as possibly opening them to receiving some of the reward money. The agency was never shy about wanting the publicity for its exploits.

The arrest of Butler was originally planned to be executed before the boat left Philadelphia. That was changed when prosecutors realized arresting him in Pennsylvania might require application to the Pennsylvania governor to approve Butler's extradition to Delaware for trial. That could have taken time and require extra expense if Butler fought the extradition.

The second choice was to wait until the boat was off the town of New Castle. Since the boundary of the State of Delaware, for twelve miles above and below New Castle, extends to the New Jersey shore, there would be no question about where the arrest took place. However, the weather intervened to change that. By the time the boat arrived in Delaware waters, there was a gale blowing out of the southwest, with thirty-mile-an-hour winds and rough water. One of the passengers that night happened to be Arley B. Magee, a Dover attorney and the vice president of the Dover and Philadelphia Navigation Company. It was agreed for the safety of the ship that the arrest would be postponed until the boat arrived in the St. Jones Creek.

At 1:00 a.m., the detectives and reporters retired to their cabins, leaving Detective Woodruff to watch Butler. The captain was requested to sound the boat's whistle three times when they arrived at their first stop at Bowers Beach, about 4:00 a.m. Butler was allowed to unload freight and conduct his normal duties until the boat left Bowers and headed to the St. Jones, half a mile to the north. There Hawkins and Lore placed Butler under arrest and took him to a cabin for questioning.

Frank Butler was described as about fifty years old, short and strongly built. He had a stubby, sandy-colored mustache and a week's growth of beard. He was dressed in his working jumpers and a closely fitting cap said to be of a type particular to river steamers.

In a straight line, Bowers Beach and the community of Lebanon, near Dover, are about six miles apart; however, the trip up the St. Jones was approximately twelve miles. By 1907, some government dredging had been done, but most of the waterway was a narrow, winding and generally shallow path through the wetlands still common to coastal Delaware. That night, the topography coupled with the continued storm resulted in an exceedingly slow five-hour trip.

The two detectives and Butler settled into stateroom No. 3 and began a marathon questioning session, during which Butler maintained his innocence. "What do you want from me?" he said. "I don't know anything about the case. If I took the lad away in a bag, before God I do not know it."[118]

The detectives asked him to repeat what he had told Dr. Marvin and the detectives during the week following the disappearance.

> *"I was working for Charles Woodall,"* he said, *"helping him move on March fourth. Besides myself, there was Verden and Caldwell, and we were removing wheat screenings from the place. We had three teams, and when we left the boy was sitting on a haystack about fifteen feet from the barn from which I loaded my team. After we had left and gone a distance of about a quarter of a mile Howard Marvin, the twenty-year-old son of Doctor Marvin, came running up to our team and asked if we had seen little Horace. Caldwell and myself, who were on one team, told him that the boy was sitting on the haystack when we left."*[119]

This was, in essence, the story told by Butler to at least five detectives, but he had also recalled the events differently at other times. His story about the bags was what interested the detectives the most. After stating he and Caldwell had taken only the three bags of screenings, Butler later said he did remember another bag, but it contained phosphate fertilizer. He denied telling Caldwell this was a bag of corks and stated that he (Butler) had taken the bag of corks to Woodall's cottage a week later.

Butler insisted that Horace was still playing on the straw stack when he and Caldwell left the farm. Caldwell was equally insistent that he had not seen Horace around the barn or straw stack at any time. Butler did admit later that, at one point, he was alone with Horace for ten minutes before Caldwell came over to the barn from the corn crib. Horace Caldwell had previously given his account of that morning's events, and Lore seemed to have settled on the differences between Caldwell and Butler's stories to narrow down the truth.

Caldwell had stated that Butler, Verden and he were working near the corn crib, when Woodall told Butler to take one of the teams to the barn and load the bags of wheat screenings, which he did. About ten minutes later, Caldwell went over to the barn to help. Butler had backed the wagon into the barn, and Caldwell said he was positive Horace Marvin was not on the haystack as he approached the barn.

Entering the barn, Caldwell saw Butler had loaded three bags of screenings on the wagon. These bags were not tied at the top. A fourth bag was on the floor of the barn, and Butler said it was full of fishing corks of the kind used for large fishing nets. Caldwell lifted the bag into the wagon and commented to Butler that it seemed heavy for being corks. Caldwell estimated it was about fifty-five pounds. Butler laughed and said he had packed them tight. This fourth bag was tied tightly at the top and was placed on the tailboard of the wagon. After the wagon was loaded, Caldwell said he asked Butler to drive, but Butler said he would rather ride on the back.[120]

At this point in the newspaper accounts there is some conflict between events, apparently as told by Caldwell. The reported versions vary, but both would have had to have been from Caldwell.

In version one, on the way to Woodall's house, they were passing through a wooded area when a bolt on the wagon broke. Butler, who was driving in this version, sent Caldwell to a nearby house for tools while he stayed to guard the items in the wagon. After the wagon was repaired and they arrived at Kitts Hummock, Caldwell noticed the bag of corks was missing. There was later speculation that Butler had hid the bag with Horace inside in the woods and went back later to bury the body. A subsequent search of the area found no trace of a grave or even disturbed earth.

In version two, Caldwell was driving, and Butler was riding on the back of the wagon, supposedly next to the bag of corks containing the body of Horace. When it fell off the wagon, Butler got off to investigate. When they arrive at Woodall's house, the bag of corks was missing. In this version, the bag turned up a week later at the home of an unidentified friend of Butler, clean and stain free.[121]

As chance would have it, Charles Woodall was a passenger on the *John P. Wilson* the night of Butler's arrest. Early in the investigation, when the authorities were looking at Butler as a suspect, Woodall had declared him innocent. That night, though, Woodall was silent. When Butler was being questioned, Woodall walked restlessly in the steamer's saloon. When a reporter later asked his opinion of the arrest, he would only say, "Butler is innocent."[122]

The boat arrived at the Lebanon landing early on Thursday, April 25, and was met by several carriages that had waited for hours in the storm. The detectives and Butler were immediately taken to the jail in Dover, where

Butler was arraigned before Justice of the Peace Edwin F. Wood, the same man who had signed his arrest warrant. After testimony from the detectives, Butler was placed in jail without bail, to await further investigation.

As New Jersey detective Frank Lore left the arraignment, he was asked by reporters if he had obtained anything important during his hours interrogating Butler. Lore, who had a reputation in New Jersey for obtaining quick confessions in major cases, answered, "Just wait. I haven't started yet."

Lore had been having a verbal sparring contest with the Pinkertons, claiming they were jealous because he had replaced them on the case and for his belief that Butler was guilty. The Pinkerton agents were in general agreement that there hadn't been enough evidence against Butler for the arrest warrant, let alone holding him for trial.

Even Detective Hawkins would make a complaint to Governor Lea about the constant interference of the Pinkerton men in the case. He charged that the Pinkerton's assistant superintendent in Philadelphia, H.H. Lintner, told Butler on the Arch Street dock not to tell the Delaware or New Jersey detectives anything. Hawkins and Lore had heard that directly from Butler.

Following Butler's early-morning commitment to jail without a formal hearing, Attorney General Richards and his deputy Daniel Hastings had planned to hold a hearing the next day, Friday. However, upon consideration, they decided it best to move it to Thursday afternoon. Their concern was that Magistrate Wood might be inclined to free Butler without strong evidence. A quick arraignment might obtain a delay from Wood to allow time for the state to get evidence and witnesses together. As requested, Magistrate Wood set a hearing for Thursday afternoon.

Word of Butler's arrest had spread, and even at the late hour a crowd had gathered at the courthouse on the Dover Green. The expert opinions expressed to reporters from both the residents and farmers were that Butler knew little about the case, but if he did know something, he wasn't telling to protect another man. The second-man theory had become popular from the talk of some people close to the case. The other side of the argument was that Butler's interrogation would result in a confession and the naming of an accomplice and the mystery would be cleared up. And that was it. Something would happen to satisfy everyone.

On Thursday morning, Hawkins and Lore returned to the jail and interrogated Butler for three hours. This time, the questioning was about every little twist and turn of the wagon trip from the Marvin barn to Woodall's house. At one point, Butler mentioned that, as they were passing by a wooded area on the property of a farmer named Dave Moore, something

Kent County Courthouse, Dover, Delaware, circa 1907. *Delaware Public Archives.*

fell off the wagon at a "boggy place" on the road. Hawkins thought this significant, as it was the same place Lucy Killen had been approached while walking home from the schoolhouse, Boggle Tree Swamp.

When Hawkins and Lore left the cell, Lore told reporters that this was one of "the simplest cases I have ever tackled, and the people will be surprised when it is all over." Hawkins added, "We have our man; of that I am certain."[123]

With all the new information, and the fact that the Kent County Grand Jury had been discharged the previous day without any action on the Marvin case, Hawkins decided to get a postponement of the hearing until the following day. Unfortunately for Hawkins, Magistrate Wood had no intention of changing the date.

The hearing was described in an understated manner by a Wilmington newspaper reporter as "while not spectacular, was dramatic in some features that attended it."[124] There were only five persons in the small courtroom: Magistrate Wood; Frank Butler; Arley Magee, the Dover lawyer and officer of the steamship company, who was representing Butler; State Detective James Hawkins; and a single reporter.

Detective Hawkins had previously spoken with Attorney General Richards, who explained to the detective how the meeting would go. Without fanfare,

Detective Hawkins rose and asked for Butler's release, telling the judge that he had been directed by the attorney general to ask for the release of the defendant because of insufficient evidence. As Magistrate Wood was about to discharge him, Butler's lawyer, Arley Magee, stood and addressed the court:

> *I want to say to you Judge, and to you Mr. Hawkins, that this is a very important case on which you have been engaged. Mr. Butler, who is a well known citizen of this State, has not objected to any test that you might subject him to because of the circumstances of having been where he was, in discharge of his lawful duty, on March 4, last.*
>
> *Now we say that if you find any evidence, at any time, that may connect Mr. Butler with this crime, whatever the time proves to be, he will be produced on his own motion or mine.*
>
> *And I want to say to you Mr. Butler that Mr. Hawkins has done what he has and they have sweated you because they had a theory and it was his plain duty to the State. You have been treated considerately, and while it has been unfortunate for you, yet the unfortunate condition surrounding this mystery has not fallen heavily upon you only.* [125]

At this point, Butler was described as being in tears. He told the court, "Gentlemen, I will not run away, if you want me, I will be ready." He then walked out of the room a free man. [126]

When Frank Butler left Dover to return to his duties on the *John P. Wilson*, the entire Marvin investigation was at its lowest point thus far. No theory of the disappearance or location of the child had been developed. After the numerous searches of the Marvin farm and surrounding areas of Kitts Hummock, there was still not a single clue that pointed to his abduction or his death. Of the dozens of reported sightings of the child, not one had shown the least connection with Horace or any potential kidnappers. After almost two months of leads from across the country and overseas, the newspapers were now limited to reporting a tenuous sighting in Wilkes Barre, Pennsylvania, and a man in Platteville, Wisconsin, who sent a letter addressed to the "Federal Government—Rhode Island," stating he had found the boy.

The few detectives appearing to work the case were the State of Delaware men and a few from the Pinkerton Baltimore office. Even the celebrated

Dover detective Frederick Murphy had lost his radiance, having been charged by Deputy Attorney General Hastings with attempting to bribe voters at the recent general election. If found guilty, Mr. Murphy could find himself in the New Castle County Workhouse sharing accommodations with several others he had sent there. Fortunately, the charges were soon dropped as being a political attack.[127]

The only ongoing activity on the case was the organization of a group of detectives and citizens to drag the Delaware Bay off the shore of the Marvin farm. The water was quite shallow there, allowing fishermen to drag nets nearly one-half a mile out at some points. This was being conducted almost two months after the boy had disappeared. Nothing was found.[128]

11

"But This Is at My Door."

By Saturday, May 4, young Horace Marvin had been missing exactly two months, and it was coincidentally his fourth birthday. The last of the promising leads on his disappearance, the arrest of Frank Butler, had vanished when the authorities realized they had no evidence to proceed with prosecution.

Dr. Marvin's neighbors had certainly done their part to help find the child. They had searched hundreds of acres of farms, marsh and woods multiple times, burned off the marsh grass and searched again and even pulled down and searched a twenty-five-foot-high straw stack to expose any clues or perhaps the body of the child.

Today, however, the farm lanes and winter fields were all but empty. Dr. Marvin had stayed at Bay Meadows that morning, avoiding the daily stacks of mail and telegrams that awaited him at the Capitol Hotel. The temperature had ranged from sixty to the mid-seventies for almost two weeks, so Dr. Marvin's neighbor Ollie Pleasanton picked up his shotgun and went out on the marsh to try to bag some ducks.

Pleasanton stepped carefully across the ground while scanning for birds. His eyes passed across tufts of marsh grass and brush and a small pond, about twenty by thirty feet, with a log on the surface of the water, but no ducks. He started to move on, but something caused him to turn back toward the pool. It wasn't a log, but the body of Horace Marvin Jr.

The body was facedown in the water, the heavy blue coat, red tam-o'-shanter knit hat and new shoes that had come with him from Sioux City clearly visible. Pleasanton quickly moved to the body, almost reflexively thinking to save the boy's life.

The tam was pulled down over the head, only a small patch of the white neck visible. There was no discoloration of the skin apparent, initially leading Pleasanton to believe the body had not been there any length of time. "I'll carry him to his father just the way he is," he thought. He carefully reached under the boy, a few strands of the golden hair visible under the cap. But as he began to raise the body from the water, he was struck by the odor of decomposition and realized that Horace had been dead and exposed to the warmth of the sun for some time. Returning the body to the water, Pleasanton ran for the farmhouse.

Dr. Marvin and his son Harvey were home when Pleasanton banged on the door. When they saw Pleasanton, he was excited and gasping for breath, and after a few moments, he managed to say, "Horace's body. In the marsh."[129] As soon as they heard the words, the three men left for the pond, stopping only long enough for the doctor to grab a white sheet. They ran as fast as they could, all being out of breath when they arrived at the pond. Dr. Marvin, now overcome at the sight of his son, broke into tears and could only communicate with Harvey and Ollie Pleasanton by waving his arms and pointing with his hands. Young Horace was wearing the clothes he wore the morning he disappeared. The little boy was dirty from the water and mud, his blue mittens still on his hands; his father gently removed the tam from his face and immediately said, "It is Horace."[130]

The two men carefully removed the body from the pond, placed it on the sheet and carefully and slowly carried it toward the house, Dr. Marvin following sorrowfully behind. At the farmyard, the body was placed in the springhouse until the authorities could be notified.

My worst fears have been realized. The finding of my poor little boy under these circumstances confirm all that I have believed concerning his fate from the very beginning. My boy was murdered. He most certainly had not been in the place where he was found but a very short time.[131]

Dr. Marvin immediately went to Dover and reported the discovery to Attorney General Richards, who set in motion the arrangements required for an autopsy and a coroner's jury to determine the cause of death. The jury would be called to meet at 10:30 the next morning, Sunday, May 5, at Bay Meadows, to allow as thorough an examination of the body as quickly as possible. Hopefully, the remaining legal requirements could be completed in a few days.

Everyone wanted answers to what had happened to Horace Marvin Jr., but the speculation didn't wait for any coroner's jury. Now the questions weren't about where Horace was, but how could he have been on Bay Meadows all along? There was no lack of opinions expressed by suspicious neighbors as well as the Pinkertons and state detectives.

Many of the residents who lived on the marsh were quick to comment on the lack of apparent harm done to the body by wildlife. The wetlands were home to buzzards and crows and other animals that scavenge for survival, and the idea that the body could have lain in the open for any length of time and remain untouched wasn't credible.

Then the other obvious argument against the boy being on the marsh was the number of searches that had been conducted. The local farmers, the various detective groups, together and separately, had crisscrossed the neighboring fields and woods, breaking through the ice, emptying wells and probing the bottom of ponds and small streams, all without success. Houses, beach shacks and boats had been searched and every neighbor questioned. If anyone knew the lay of the land at Kitts Hummock, it was the men who lived on it, and nothing had been seen.

There were the public comments by several of the searchers, including Dr. Marvin. In a statement to a Wilmington newspaper shortly after the discovery of his son's body, the doctor said he and Pinkerton detective Bearce had stood at, or near, the very pond where Horace was eventually found. But neither had seen anything, not even his bright red tam.[132]

But the most curious was the lack of any fire damage to young Horace's clothing when the body was found. The marsh grass had been burned off just four weeks before, with searchers closely following the flames as they progressed across the fields. No trace of Horace had been seen then, and no trace of the fire was on his clothing now. The autopsy and the coroner's jury investigation were expected to answer these questions and find who was responsible for the death of Horace Marvin Jr.

The evening of Horace's discovery, Dr. Marvin started to investigate the condition of his son and removed the sheet from the body. He removed the cap covering the face, but then stopped. Aware that the coroner's jury should be the ones doing the examination, and that he did not wish to see his son in this condition, he said to his son Harvey, "Oh, I'll let the postmortem doctors do this. I have been strong many times for other people, but this is at my door."[133]

State deputy attorney general Satterfield was appointed to be prosecuting attorney and immediately began selecting the members of the coroner's jury. Dr. Lemuel A.H. Bishop would conduct the actual postmortem. The autopsy staff, all of whom were medical doctors, consisted of Dr. Wilson, who would be chief of the team; Wilbur D. Burton, a Kent County physician; E.F. O'Day of Little Creek; and Alfred Robin, a bacteriologist for the City of Wilmington. Dr. William F. Hoey, of Frederica, would be present as a witness.

Other jury members included the following:[134]

Eldad L. Clarke	jury foreman, a Dover merchant and foreman of the sitting Kent County Grand Jury
Herman Taylor	jury secretary, newspaperman and former state assemblyman
William G. Postles	former mayor of Dover
Benjamin M. Moore	former county commissioner
John C. Hopkins	jury commissioner
Heuston A. Culbreth	
Thomas Muncey	
Franklin Temple	
R.P.G. Wilson	
Gilbert Marvel	
Dr. James Martin	
Nathaniel White	

Foreman Clarke was quoted as saying that the inquiry would be most searching:

> *The jury is not going to proceed on anybody's dictation.....No matter what the sentiment is this jury can be relied on to not leave anything undone, to leave no loophole....I believe we have the best jury possible to get in Delaware...and the State is more than willing for them to cover every detail and will heartily co-operate with them to that effect.*[135]

12

QUESTIONS

In Dover and neighboring towns, the fate of little Horace Marvin was discussed yesterday by throngs on the streets, by men standing around everywhere in groups, by travelers, drivers and automobilists meeting by the roadside, and by congregations of neighbors in each other's houses. It was the meat and drink yesterday and for one Sunday in lower Delaware the highly regarded public worship suffered.[136]

Several hours before the 10:00 a.m. time for the coroner's jury to be sworn in, a constant procession of wagons and men on horseback could be seen stretching west on the long lane to the Marvin farm. Long rows of tethered horses and a crowd estimated at 1,500 people filled the lawn, the barnyard and fields adjacent to the shed where the inquest would be held. It seemed the only persons missing on this Sunday morning were the three men who had been central to this story from the beginning: Woodall, Butler and Caldwell.[137]

All the required officials were present on the Marvin farm, and an expedited formal inquest was conducted by the coroner, Joseph Callaway. Under Delaware law, Callaway had the primary responsibility to investigate all cases in which a person died an unnatural death or the condition surrounding the death could not be determined. Dr. Marvin testified that the body was that of his son Horace Marvin Jr., and Oliver Pleasanton then related his finding of the body. These were the only two statements taken at this time, solely for the purpose of establishing the identity of the body.

Newspaper image of the place where Horace was found, with a photo insert of Ollie Pleasanton. *From the* Evening Journal (Wilmington, DE).

The jury was then taken to where the body was found and allowed to see the terrain the four-year-old boy would have had to cross to reach the pond. The men walked across the stubble of a large wheat field, crossed a four-foot-deep ditch and navigated through a barbed wire fence before coming to the pond. That was assuming the child traveled on a straight path from the straw stack. That direct line was later measured by John C. Hopkins, a civil engineer, who placed the distance at 1,760 feet, or exactly one-third of a mile, northeast of the stack. This trip raised doubt in the minds of several jurors about the child's death being an accident.

Other jurors, however, were impressed with the accounts of several farmers who had helped search for the boy. At the time of the jury visit, it was reported there was about seven inches of water in the pond. However, just a few feet away was a much deeper hole that was full of water. The previous searchers said that, at the time of their search, there was much less water in that hole. It was pointed out that just two nights before the jury's visit, there had been a heavy rain, which would account for the current volume of water. This suggested to several jury members that the boy could have fallen through the ice and died, becoming trapped under the ice, and periodic rains could have moved the body.

During the nine weeks of searching for Horace, the various state and private detective agencies repeatedly told reporters of the thoroughness of their examination of the Marvin farm, outbuildings and marsh lands. Now, before the jurors, State Detective Gillis and Pinkerton superintendent Dimaio called several farmers who had participated in those searches.

They all admitted that they had been in the vicinity of the pond on several occasions, but none would say they had actually dragged the bottom.[138] The jury then returned to the shed for the postmortem, already full of members of the public, eager to watch the event.

In 1907, the autopsy as a means of obtaining information on the cause of death was in its infancy. It wasn't that people hadn't studied the dead. It was well known that early Egyptians removed and preserved some internal organs of the deceased, but this was part of burial rites rather than a medical procedure. Other early types of physical examination of a corpse developed to educate medical students or to study the effects of a particular disease. However, none of these were specifically intended to obtain information about the cause of death.

One of the earliest autopsies to determine cause of a death was that of Roman emperor Julius Caesar following his assassination in the Roman Senate on March 15, 44 BCE. The physician conducting the autopsy found Caesar had been stabbed twenty-three times, but a single wound that had pierced his aorta caused his death.

For over 1,900 years, the progress of determining the cause of a death of an individual, or identifying the person who may have killed them, scarcely advanced. It wasn't until 1908 that Scotland Yard created the first medical examiner with the Office of the Forensic Pathologist. This position, under the direction of a medically trained person, was charged with investigating the cause of all unnatural deaths, including accidents, murders and suicides.

The first police crime laboratory wasn't established until 1910 in Lyon, France, at the suggestion of Dr. Edmond Locard. Dr. Locard's work led him to develop what has become known as the "exchange principle," which says it is impossible for a criminal to leave a crime scene without leaving behind some trace of his presence that could be used to identify him. This application of scientific knowledge to solving crimes would lead to the development of the field of forensic science.[139] Of course, little of the technology and scientific methods being slowly developed around the world would have any effect on the case of young Horace Marvin Jr.

The witness depositions were considered by the members of the inquest, who unanimously decided that the cause of the death of Horace Marvin was unknown, and an autopsy would be needed to attempt to determine the cause. The findings were certified and signed by the coroner, who immediately delivered them, and the pro forma custody of the body, to Deputy Attorney General Satterfield.

Satterfield then transferred custody to Dr. James H. Wilson, a member of the staff of the New Castle County Hospital at Farnhurst, near Wilmington. In normal circumstances, a formal autopsy would have been conducted in a more private setting than a farm shed, but the need for a quick burial preempted any routine procedures.[140]

It began with an examination of the general appearance of the child's body. Little Horace was still dressed in the clothes he was reportedly wearing on the morning of his disappearance. The red knit cap and heavy reefer coat were cut away, removed and examined. In the pockets of the coat were a small purse containing four bright pennies that rolled out on the table and three small dolls that the child was known to carry with him. A small handkerchief was in a pocket of the shirt.

The doctor's attention was drawn to the clean condition of the clothing. There was a lack of significant mud staining, and the good condition of the shoes and stockings was of particular note. This point—the condition of the shoes—led Eldad L. Clarke, the jury foreman, to request they be sent to a leather expert for examination. Each additional item—his Buster Brown suit, blue overalls and underwear—was carefully cut from the body, removed and examined, but nothing was found that might indicate anything that may have caused injury or death of the child.

One question about the condition of the body was quickly answered. Immediately after the discovery, it appeared to be in a well-preserved condition, challenging the opinion that it may have been on the marsh any length of time. However, the physical examination found more advanced decomposition of the body had occurred than would have been expected if the boy had recently died.

The face was swollen and discolored, the body having no outward injuries visible except for a slight abrasion over the left eye and a big blood discoloration on one side of the neck, which was found not to extend below the surface of the skin. While neither of these were considered significant by Dr. Wilson, there were reports that other physicians were not in agreement. A large stripe several inches wide was found running across the child's back; initially, the mark was thought to be caused by the wheel of a wagon, as this had been an early consideration. However, it was found to have been caused by the swelling of the body against the belt of the boy's Buster Brown suit.

The entire body showed signs of having been part of the time above water and part of the time below water. However, the lungs were found to be collapsed and containing very little water, eliminating drowning as the cause of death. The liver was the only organ that appeared unusual; it was described as "congested."

There was surprise at the lack of food in the stomach. The family had reported that Horace had eaten an egg, bread and some oatmeal the morning of his disappearance. This led to a rumor that the boy had been starved to death before being thrown into the pool. Dr. Wilson stated that he believed this indicated that the child had lived between twenty-four and forty-eight hours after his last meal.

Wilson added that no one could say exactly when the child died, but he estimated possibly four to five weeks. However, the periods of recent warm daytime temperatures, and where the body may have been located, would have had an influence on the estimate.

A complete examination of the stomach contents could not be performed outside of a laboratory, so the stomach and intestines were removed and placed in the custody of Dr. Albert Robin, the Wilmington bacteriologist. Robin was also a professor of pathology at Temple Medical College in Philadelphia. His examination would also help determine the cause and time of death.

Attorney General Richards was later asked if the examination by Dr. Robin was prompted by a suspicion of poisoning. "None whatever, and I did it simply because of the national interest in the case and to guard against any possible contingencies."[141] He added that he did not believe there would be any future revelations, and at the present time he knew of no suspicions against anyone who might have caused the death of Horace Marvin.

At this point in the inquest, with no evidence of violence on the boy, the jury tried to reconstruct the last actions of the child that would have placed him where the body was found. The only factor noted in the reported accounts of the inquest suggest that, at some point early on the morning of March 4, someone had told the children about the large body of water to the east of the farmhouse. The presence of sharks and mermaids were mentioned, which may have prompted Horace to go in search of the water once he was alone in the farmyard.[142]

After completion of the autopsy, Dr. Wilson adjourned the jury, with instructions to reconvene Friday, May 10, at 10:00 a.m. in the Kent County

Court House. The delay was to allow Dr. Robin time to finish his examination and prepare his report, which was expected to take a week.

At the close of the autopsy, the body was turned over to the undertaker, a Mr. Pritchett, and Dr. Marvin. It was placed in a white coffin and taken to the parlor, where Horace's aunt, Mrs. Standish, and his grandmother Flora Swift had made wreaths of apple blossoms, plum branches and ferns. A brief burial service was conducted by two local Methodist ministers, Reverends Hugh Kelso of Magnolia and E.H. Nelson of Camden. Interment of the body followed at sunset, under a tree in front of the farmhouse.

Standing at the foot of the low mound of earth covered with wreaths, Dr. Marvin told a reporter that he intended to sell Bay Meadows and take Horace's remains back to Iowa. "I cannot rest in peace on the place that has brought me so much sorrow, and I'll be glad when I quit it....I cannot get away from it quickly enough."[143]

13

JUDGMENT

I n the days leading up to the meeting of the coroner's jury, the autopsy
was the only topic of conversation in Dover. State detectives James
Hawkins and Harry Gillis were as divided as everyone else on the results
thus far. Hawkins could not agree with the possibility of young Horace dying
a natural death. It was "simply out of the question," he said in response to
an inquiry from a Wilmington *Evening-Journal* reporter. On March 4, the
day of the disappearance, Hawkins and Samuel Saxton of Dover had gone
to the pond where the boy would be found two months later and found ice
thick enough to support a 108-pound man.

Detective Hawkins testified:

> *On the thirteenth and fourteenth of the same month* [March] *Mr.
> Pleasanton, father of the man who found the body, waded through the pond
> and with poles, on the ends of which were sharp pointed iron hooks, prodded
> every inch of the ground. That there was no body there at that time I am
> certain. We also raked all the ditches in the vicinity but found nothing that
> would indicate that the missing boy was thereabouts. I do not place any
> credence in the belief that the boy was not kidnapped.*[144]

Detective Gillis, however, was just as certain that the boy died of starvation
at the pool while searchers were within feet of him. Gillis had been one of
the first to see the body after it was recovered and told the reporter that "it
showed every indication of starvation, and no evidence of foul play. The

baby's mittens were on his hands just as they had been placed there by his father two months before, there was no disarrangement of the clothing and the little corpse was in an advanced state of decomposition."[145]

Gillis was certain the searchers had not examined the depression in the ground where the body was later found. He also stated that there was no indication that the grass surrounding the pond had been burned, as commonly reported.[146]

The following day, Franklin and Ollie Pleasanton were quoted in the *Evening-Journal* as being anxious to set the coroner's jury straight on a point of their testimony. They had said that the spot where the body was found had been carefully searched by both of them, and if a body had been there, they would have found it. They also said that "Doctor Marvin and Superintendent Bearce, of the Pinkertons, had also burned the grass almost at the very spot."

Furthermore, in a somewhat confusing statement, they said that there was a "hitherto undiscovered deep place at the southeast extreme of this marshy place, and that at the bottom of that the body was imbedded in the mud. They only searched it with long sticks." The heavy thunderstorm the night before the body was found had "stirred up and floated the child's body… starting it northeast until it had floated into only seventeen inches of water, where it stuck and was found."[147]

However, the opinions of the experts held little weight in the court of public opinion. With four days before the meeting of the coroner's jury, the Dover street corners, barrooms and hotel lobbies were busy with their own examination of evidence.

The general belief in Dover was that the inquest would agree with the opinion of the physicians at the autopsy that the child had wandered onto the marsh, where he died of exposure, and the body was preserved under ice until it was free to rise to the surface. But it didn't make sense that the body had remained in the same spot for nine weeks. The fields had been covered with ice, thawed during the many days of warm weather, then dried out and filled during the periods of often heavy rains, not to mention walked and burned over by hundreds of men deliberately looking for any trace of the boy. To the Kitts Hummock fishermen and farmers, the boy could have been kidnapped and held at an unknown place until the fear of discovery led the captors to starve the child and leave his body in a place it was certain to be found.

The counter opinion was the theory that the boy had been accidentally killed and hidden somewhere until the body could be taken to the pond.

There were opinions on who might have been responsible, but these fell apart when no good evidence could be discovered concerning any of the suspects.

Of course, the Pinkertons, through Superintendent Dimaio, would always stand by their belief that the boy had simply wandered away across the marsh until he fell through an air hole in the ice and remained there until found nine weeks later.

And as if this story needed another twist, late Saturday evening, a gray-haired old man appeared at the Marvin home. He wouldn't give a name but said he had traveled from Lincoln, Nebraska, to help the doctor solve the case. He had walked the entire distance from Dover in the rain and wanted to remain a few days. Dr. Marvin gave him a meal and a place to sleep, and the mystery man disappeared the following morning.[148]

The family also declined to comment on rumors around the town and mentioned in some newspaper reports that Dr. Marvin was going to sell Bay Meadows and return to the West. The doctor was worn out by the ordeal of the past few days and was enjoying the first sound sleep he had in the past nine weeks.[149]

On May 6, the day after the autopsy, the Wilmington *Evening Journal* ran an interview with the former coroner Alfred D. Vandever. He told the reporter that he did not believe the body of the Marvin boy had been dead forty hours. If the body had been exposed in the marsh for nine weeks, Vandever said, due to the sun and the hot days in March, there would be nothing remaining except the clothing.

If the body had been in the pond the entire time, there would have been an accumulation of sediment on the body "from a quarter to a half inch thick." And regarding the boy's stomach, Vandever believed that the presence of, or lack of, food would have had no significance regarding the time of death.[150]

The members of the coroner's jury began filtering into Dover early on May 10, and the press was ready with questions about what was going to happen. Dr. Robin's report on the examination of the young boy's stomach had been received by Attorney General Richards, but he declined comment until it had been presented to the jury. The rumor was that it did not find any poison.

Another more disturbing rumor was that the inquest was to be held behind closed doors. A reason given was supposedly due to the large number of witnesses, but that had not occurred in any previous inquests, and if it was true, the newspapermen were expected to be allowed in.[151]

Dr. William Hoey and Detective Fred Minner were in town, and both met with Coroner Calloway and Deputy Attorney General Satterfield. Hoey had attended the autopsy as a courtesy and believed himself able to offer his thoughts on the case as a private citizen. Not mincing his words, he stated, "There are possibilities in all things, but a possibility and probability present two altogether different conditions. I do not believe that the child's body had ever been on that marsh, in the shallow water in which it was found, or which characterized that entire pool, for any nine weeks." He admitted the lack of signs of violence against the child but noted that it was impossible for anyone to tell when a person had been smothered to death.[152]

There had also been two weeks of extremely warm weather right after the disappearance, and Dr. Hoey felt the inquest should hear from a weather expert. "The only way a body could have been kept at the bottom during that time was to have it anchored."[153]

Detective Minner was equally adamant, declaring that he had made a search of the pool and had watched others drag the water and use poles with barbed ends, all with no results. "That body was put there about two weeks ago," he said. "I'll swear it was not there when we searched, and we worked through a hot spell when we had to shed our coats and collars."[154]

The Saturday, May 11 session of the inquest was supposed to begin at 10:00 a.m., but prior to the start several of the jurors met and garnered enough votes to control the deliberations. They entered the meeting room, where juror James Martin made a motion that the room should be cleared, including newsmen. The stated reason was that the jurors might be embarrassed asking about some details of the crime and might feel more comfortable without the public being present and only one witness at a time being called. The motion passed, and Foreman Clarke ordered everyone out of the room except State Detective James Hawkins, serving as the sergeant-at-arms, who called the witnesses.[155]

Someone then pointed out to the jury that two of their members were employed as newspaper correspondents. It seemed reasonable that if they remained, everyone present in the room should be obligated not to reveal the proceedings but allow the foreman to publish the notes of court stenographer Hardesty at the close of the inquest. Juror Fluke demanded an oath of secrecy from everyone in the room, to which a Wilmington newspaperman, W.T. Price, refused and left the room.

The reporters who were ejected contacted their respective newspapers and formulated a respectful response. It appears it was never considered by the jury. The reporting of the inquest examinations was likely obtained by questioning witnesses and other persons who had been in the room. The reporters' protest is printed at the end of this chapter.[156]

But the most unusual event of the day's session occurred just before the jury was called to order. Coroner Calloway was approached by jury member Robert Wilson, who informed him that, on the preceding day, he and several other men went to the pond on the Marvin farm where little Horace had been found. Wilson said he had gone to collect a sample of water from the pond to see if it was salt or fresh, which he deemed important regarding the condition of the boy's body. While looking for something to use to get a sample, Wilson said he remembered seeing a whiskey bottle there on the day of the autopsy. Upon finding the bottle, he opened it and discovered it contained a piece of paper with four names written on it and a date, "March 10, 1907." The date was six days after the child's disappearance. The names were later determined to be John Burns, Robert Passwaters, John Smith and James Sylvester. All of the men were young farmers from the Milford, Delaware area, about twenty miles south of Dover.[157]

The bottle and its contents were turned over to Attorney General Richards, who indicated he would investigate. Several members of the coroner's jury who lived in Milford indicated they would drive through the Milford neighborhood before coming to Dover the following morning. With the conclusion of the inquest in a few days, this question was either ignored by the attorney general or never pursued by the press.

The highly unusual action of closing the proceedings to the people and reporters, and the evident secrecy of the names in the bottle, created a suspicion among the public that the authorities might be trying to suppress some unfavorable information about the case. Their suspicions would remain throughout the inquest.[158]

By 11:00 a.m., the inquest room had been cleared of all unauthorized people, and the business of hearing from the witnesses began. The first was

Dr. Wilson, chief of the autopsy staff. He presented a detailed report of his examination of the skeletal system and soft tissue of the child. Wilson had done a microscopic examination of the heart and a cursory examination of the stomach, the latter having been examined in detail by Dr. Robin, whose report would follow. Under questioning of the jury members, Dr. Wilson stated that Horace Marvin's death could not have been caused by anything but suffocation, or perhaps strangulation.

Dr. Robin could not be present for the inquest, but his analysis of Horace Marvin's stomach contents was read to the jury by Dr. Wilson. It stated that chemical and microscopic analysis of the stomach showed the presence of glutenous matter and food particles indicating the boy had eaten a light breakfast and died before it had passed through the body. Robin testified his last meal had been oatmeal, parts of an egg and small particles of bread. The bread had not been eaten all at once but had been broken into small pieces.

"In the absence of any other cause," Robin wrote, he believed the boy had met an accidental death from exposure, and "death could have occurred, and probably did occur, within six to twelve hours after eating his last meal."[159]

Dr. Robin also testified that as a physician he had seen several dead bodies and that from the examination of young Horace, he concluded the body had been in the water between six and eight weeks. This point was corroborated by other physicians.

The contents of Horace's last meal had been mentioned previously, but Dr. Marvin and the ladies of the household testified to the facts later in the inquest. Dr. Marvin also added that little Horace had been ill and vomited the night before his disappearance, emptying his stomach.

At the time of the initial examination of the body at the autopsy, it was noted by several persons that the shoes on the child were in very good condition. Believing the body may have been in water for an extended period, Attorney General Richards had the shoes sent for examination by a leather expert. The examination was conducted by John Paris Jr., a shoe and leather expert from Wilmington, the city having several major producers of finished leather. He gave his testimony before the jury.

Paris's conclusion was that the shoes could not have been under water for more than a week. Several jurors tried to get Paris to state that the shoes had positively not been soaking in the pond for two months, which he refused to state. He did say that, depending on the chemical preparations used to finish some leathers, the shoes could have withstood a prolonged soaking and still be in good condition.[160]

Three of the four men who had been working around the Marvin farmyard the day Horace disappeared were called by the inquest. Charles Woodall, Horace Caldwell and Frank Butler were the last to see the boy as they drove their wagons off the property; however, Butler held the most interest at the courthouse. He had been arrested as a prime suspect in the boy's disappearance before having the charges dropped, and some people were still suspicious about his involvement.

Butler's answers to the jury questioning were described as brief and pointed, but he did not refuse to answer some questions as he initially had following his earlier arrest. He repeated his answers about his actions and movements on March 4 and that he last saw little Horace playing on the straw stack. He did remark that when the children were in the yard that morning, he had overheard Dr. Marvin speaking to them, telling them there was a big bay to the east and it was full of boats and big fish. Butler thought that may have influenced the direction the child had later taken.[161] It was late Saturday night before the inquest adjourned until the following day.

The Sunday, May 12 session opened with Juror Sawtelle making a motion that the newspaper reporters be allowed back into the hearing room. He said the correspondents were still getting their information accurately and that someone in the inquest must be breaking their promise not to discuss the proceeding outside the room. A vote was taken on the motion, but no public announcement was made of the result, nor were there any reports that the ban had been lifted in any newspaper accounts.

The superintendent of the Philadelphia Pinkerton office, H.W. Bearce, was called to the inquest. He had just arrived that morning and briefly went to the Marvin farm. The finding of the body on the farm agreed with the Pinkerton theory that the boy had just wandered off. In his testimony, he said that he and Dr. Marvin had burned off grass on the farm but the flames had not reached the spot where Horace was found.[162]

Frank Lore, the New Jersey detective who had attempted to track several leads over the past weeks, was questioned. Lore was of the opposite opinion from the Pinkertons, believing that the boy had either been killed accidentally or was murdered by a person or persons unknown and the body placed in the pool. Several jurors questioned him on the latter point, even recalling the previous day's testimony of John Paris on the effect of water on the boy's shoes.

Related testimony was heard from Charles Treidler of Dover, who was called as a clothing expert. He told the inquest that Horace had enough clothing on him to keep the body weighed down, even without being anchored in place.

After two days of questions, the jury adjourned. They were instructed to return the following day to deliberate and try to decide what had happened to Horace Marvin Jr.

On Monday, May 13, the fifteen voting members of the coroner's jury met in their room in the Kent County Court House and immediately found they were divided into three opinions on the case. Twelve votes were needed for a legal verdict.

> First: Little Horace had wandered from the barnyard to the spot where he was found and died from exposure. This view had the majority of support. Second: The child had met with violence by person or persons unknown. Third: The cause of death was unknown and could not be determined from the evidence presented to the inquest.[163]

The jury repeatedly discussed the testimony and voted, with no change until the twelfth ballot. Then one voter changed their vote to "Death from exposure by hands unknown to the jury," meaning the boy had been kidnapped and held but then set free and died from exposure. The juror supported the reworded ballot because Dr. Wilson gave testimony that the boy had been held captive for five to six weeks and died from exposure. There was enough doubt about the remaining facts to make him change his ballot.

The balloting resumed, with several breaks, until the jury sent for Deputy Attorney General Satterfield. He had left the room earlier and was asked to return to the inquest room and discuss the duties of a coroner's jury. According to one reporter, he appeared with several law books and a little night school was started in Delaware law. At 11:00 p.m., the jury finally agreed on a verdict of "Death from exposure."[164]

On Thursday, May 16, 1907, the Wilmington *Evening Journal* published an editorial about the verdict:

> The coroner's jury of Kent county after considering in secret the testimony concerning the death of little Horace Marvin rendered a verdict that the boy died from exposure. A great mass of evidence was heard, but what it was the public has no definite means of knowing. The death from exposure theory will probably finally be accepted by most people as logical. Had the jury, however, permitted the evidence to become public in a proper manner any lingering doubt about this case might be dismissed.[165]

Given the secrecy surrounding the hearing and the difficulty the coroner's jury had in reaching an agreement on the verdict, the newspapers' suspicion of lingering doubt among the public in the manner of young Horace's death might seem warranted. However, there is no indication this was the case. In fact, there had been a recent precedent that may have contributed to the public acceptance of the decision. This was a death in New Castle, Delaware, almost four years earlier that had been referred to as "The Proudfit Mystery."

In the May 9, 1904 edition of the Wilmington *Evening Journal*, a small article appeared on page four under the curious heading "The Proudfit Mystery Solved." It's likely many of the men on the jury had seen it, and it may have even been discussed in their deliberations. The article reported that, around 12:30 on the afternoon of May 8, 1904, a local fisherman named Charles Congers noticed something floating in the Delaware River about two hundred yards off Battery Park, in New Castle. Congers and his colleagues agreed that it appeared to be a body, and the incoming tide would soon have it close enough to the beach to be secured.

Once the body was on shore, it was readily apparent it was that a man but in such a poor condition that immediate identification was impossible. The deceased was wearing a lightweight summer shirt, gray trousers and tan shoes. He had no identification or possessions on him except an open-faced nickel pocket watch. The hands had stopped at 4:23, the likely time the deceased had entered the river. And it was also notable that there was a significant amount of clay sticking to the clothing.

While it was not possible to identify the man, the locals recalled that, six months earlier, on November 3, 1903, a New Castle resident, John W. Proudfit, had gone canoeing on the river but disappeared, leaving only his canoe and his hat behind. Proudfit was living with an aunt, New Castle resident Hettie Smith, at the time of his disappearance, who identified the watch, and the description of the clothing on the body, as his.

A coroner's jury was empaneled, and the verdict was determined to have been accidental drowning. It was the general belief that the gap of six months between Proudfit falling into the river and his resurfacing was that the body sank into one of the many clay holes in the river bottom. New Castle had a commercial brickmaking business at the time and obtained the raw clay by dredging the Delaware River off the town shore. The body sank to the bottom and became stuck in one of these holes in May 1903 but was dislodged when clay dredging resumed a few weeks before the body was seen on the surface.[166]

THE REPORTERS PROTEST AT BEING BANNED FROM THE INQUEST

To the Honorable Joseph Calloway, coroner of Kent county, and the honorable members of the coroner's jury in the case of Horace N. Marvin Jr., deceased;

Gentlemen: We, the undersigned, duly accredited representatives of the undersigned newspapers and press associations, have been advised and instructed by our offices to request that we be admitted for the hearing of testimony in the above inquest, and be excluded for the deliberations of the jury. We are further advised to ask this for three reasons.

First, that it has never been the custom anywhere in the United States to exclude duly accredited newspaper representatives from any court or investigation of a death.

Second, that the interest in this case has spread through two continents, and is, therefore, not purely local; and that the jury is doing a great injustice to withhold this information from the public until such time as it sees fit to release it, and,

Third, that there are already representatives of the press present who are bound by the positions they hold as reporters to publish the news, even though they abide by the injunction of the jury not to print the testimony as it is given. The advantage they thus obtain is manifestly unfair, particularly to the newspapers who have gone to the trouble and expense to send staff representatives here.[167]

14

EPILOGUE

I n the days immediately following the discovery of Horace Marvin's body, American newspapers, large and small, hit the streets with over 150 articles, extras and special editions. This was approximately twice the number published right after his disappearance.[168] The nation, and much of the world, had followed the daily reports of the false clues and mistaken sightings and the apparent incompetence of the dozens of private and professional detectives who couldn't solve the mystery of his disappearance or, apparently, his death. However, once the coroner's jury made its determination, the story quickly dropped from the news.

On May 18, the Pinkerton Agency sent a bill to Governor Lea in the amount of $2,000 for services to the state in the investigation of the Horace Marvin Jr. disappearance. Oddly enough, that was the exact amount appropriated by the legislature. Dr. Marvin would have received a similar bill for the detectives he had hired, but the total amount he spent was never publicly disclosed.

The cost of the inquest into Horace Marvin's death was the responsibility of the Kent County government, and its governing body, called the Levy Court,[169] had to approve the expenses. On July 3, after some debate on certain individual items in the $280.00 bill, the commissioners agreed that in the end, "The Court thought it best to sustain and fully endorse the attorney general's department and uphold their determination to spare no reasonable expense."[170] That included everything from the $81.00 for the stenographer, down to $30.00 for the surgeons' bills and $4.00 per jury member for each day of the inquest.

The Marvin family gradually resumed their lives, getting their home in order and starting to make their farm productive. Dr. Marvin slowly regained his health and decided he was not moving back to Iowa.

In August, Harvey Marvin made a trip to South Dakota, probably to attend to the sale of his farm and cattle ranch. He told a reporter that Dr. Marvin would be making a short visit to South Dakota in September. The doctor would be bringing with him the remains of his son Horace, to be interred next to his mother in the Logan Park Cemetery. Afterward he would return to Dover. Harvey said the reports of East Coast reporters that his father would leave Delaware to return to Sioux City were incorrect.[171]

If Dr. Marvin took his September trip to South Dakota, he probably planned a quick return to Delaware. On October 1, a new member came into the Marvin family when Howard Marvin and his wife, Emma, welcomed a son to the Bay Meadow farm where they were living. The boy was promptly named Horace Newel Marvin III, after young Horace who had died just six months earlier.

Unfortunately, the child died on March 11, 1908, from undisclosed causes. This led to the body of the young infant of Howard and Emma, and the remains of Horace buried on Bay Meadows, both being reinterred in the Lakeside Cemetery in Dover.

On Friday, November 8, 1907, a Sioux City, Iowa newspaper[172] put a report on the newswire that it had learned from a source in Dover that on Thursday Dr. Marvin had married his mother-in-law, Flora M. Thornton-Swift. The news was picked up and reprinted in several East Coast papers, including the *Washington (D.C.) Times* and the Wilmington *Evening Journal*.

There had been rumors for several days that the wedding had taken place, but reporters could find no record of a license at the Dover courthouse. Although the family attempted to keep the news secret, it was confirmed on Friday by a source reportedly in the town of Livingston, Delaware. The wedding had occurred at a parsonage in that community, a few miles from Dover. However, there are no contemporary records of a town by the name of Livingston in Delaware in 1907.

It was said no objections to the marriage were raised by the doctor's two older sons, Dr. Harvey Marvin or Howard Marvin. The paper noted that the boys' father was sixty-three and had rapidly declined in health following

Horace's death, and he just wished to live quietly on a farm and be comforted in his last days.

Mrs. Swift had stood by the doctor during the search for Horace and made him rest and eat. She reportedly had been his constant companion during those days, and relatives of Dr. Marvin had approved the third marriage. The *Washington Times* story was even more detailed, repeating the basic information of the disappearance of Horace and reprising information about Mrs. Swift being a spiritualist and her having received several "revelations" during the two-month search for Horace.[173]

The *Ocala (FL) Evening Star*, November 11, 1907 edition, ran a small front-page notice of the wedding but with the headline:

MARRIED HIS MOTHER-IN-LAW
Queer Matrimonial Stunt of Dr. Horace Marvin, Who Has Already Received Much Newspaper Notoriety.

And on November 15, the *Washington Herald*, which had covered the disappearance from the beginning, wrote: "Dr. Horace Marvin, the loss of whose little boy created such a sensation throughout the land about a year ago, has married his mother-in-law. Is this another bid for condolence and sympathy?"[174]

Apparently, the nation's newspaper editors felt they had used enough ink on Horace Marvin. Evidently sharing the feelings of the *Ocala Evening Star*, few picked up the marriage article, and those that did usually limited it to a short item, often placed on an inside page.

The sudden appearance of the story wasn't good news for Dr. Marvin. On November 9, he told reporters in Dover that the accounts from Sioux City, Iowa, that he had married his mother-in-law "are without the least foundation." and were "false in every particular."[175] According to the doctor, Flora Swift had been in Providence, Rhode Island, for the past two months with young John Marvin, the brother of Horace. John was attending school in Providence. This was quickly confirmed.

To further prove the report was incorrect, Marvin stated what the local press already knew. No marriage license had been issued to the couple in the Dover courthouse. And according to a reporter's conversation with the family, there was certainly no probability of such a marriage taking place.

It was a fitting close to the terrible year for the Marvin family that there had to be one final newspaper article connected to their name. On December 26, George Pinebird was arrested in Philadelphia for passing a bad check and was locked up in the Central Station jail. Pinebird was well known to the police as a man who had claimed on multiple occasions to have knowledge of the location of young Horace Marvin. All his tips proved to be a waste of police time and manpower.[176] It may be remembered, on March 16, a Joseph Pinebird of Philadelphia reported to police he had information about a possible sighting of Horace Marvin. This also turned out to be nothing. It's not known if George and Joseph were two individuals or the same man, misidentified by reporters.

The New Year's Eve optimism of better days in 1908 was marked in Delaware with activities ranging from quiet religious observances and family dinners to the carnival atmosphere of thousands of people who gathered in Wilmington with shouts, bells, whistles and the occasional skyward pistol shot. The only thing new was the presence of one "venturesome automobilist [who] sounded the reveille on a bugle as he rode up and down in a chariot of red."[177]

Delawareans who may have ventured to New York City would have had the opportunity to see a new addition to their four-year-old New Year's Eve celebration in Times Square. While maybe not as flashy as a man in a red automobile blowing a bugle, the city added a seven-hundred-pound, five-foot-diameter iron and wood ball, covered in one hundred twenty-five-watt light bulbs. This illuminated orb would actually be slowly lowered to mark the beginning of the new year to the amazement of those gathered below.[178]

Dr. Marvin Weds the Mother of His Second Wife.

Readers of the January 10, 1908 edition of the Wilmington *Evening Journal* newspaper could be excused for double checking the date on the masthead that night. Just a few weeks earlier, they had seen a similar headline that turned out to be an attempt at a joke. However, this time the date, and the headline, were accurate. Even so, it still might have remained a secret, as it was probably intended to be, if not for the City of New York.

Sometime in 1907, the New York City government realized the office that issued marriage licenses was overloaded and out of date. A reorganization was planned, and a new Marriage Bureau was opened at the end of the year in the city hall building. Applicants now had an orderly process to fill out the required paperwork, pay the one-dollar fee, have an interview with the city clerk, Mr. Scully, and be issued their license.

The new office was praised by the applicants as being efficient, with courteous employees who would answer questions and even help them to fill out the forms. An efficient and popular branch of any city bureaucracy was enough to attract the attention of the press, and soon reporters were eager to get first-person stories from the soon-to-be newlyweds. The reporters also noticed that hanging around the Marriage Bureau allowed them to see the applications and get a story on which public figure or socialite might be planning a walk down the aisle. That led to a sharp-eyed reporter recognizing the names of Dr. Horace N. Marvin and Mrs. Flora Melina Swift, and any hope of secrecy vanished.

The couple visited the bureau on Thursday morning, January 9; filled out their paperwork together; and were both closely examined by Mr. Scully, who was unaware of their recent notoriety. It was reported that they were the most noteworthy couple on record thus far at the bureau.

On the application, Dr. Marvin gave occupation as a farmer and physician, place of birth as Ohio and his residence as Dover, Delaware. He gave his age as sixty-two, his wife to be sixty. He listed his two previous marriages and his children's names and ages.

Mrs. Swift stated she was born in Franzburg, New York, her father being Albert Thornton. Her maiden name was Flora Melina Thornton, Swift being her second husband's name, and she was currently a resident of Brookline, Massachusetts.

At 1:00 p.m. the couple finished their interview and left city hall accompanied by the bride's daughter, Mrs. Miles Standish, and her husband, and Mr. and Mrs. Howard Marvin. They drove to the Church of the Transfiguration, also known as "The Little Church around the Corner," at 1 East 29th Street, where they were married by Reverend Dr. George C. Houghton. Afterward the wedding party took a train to Dover.[179]

The maiden name of Dr. Marvin's new wife was Flora Melina Thornton. She was reportedly born in Farnsburg, New York, on August 25, 1847, but there is no record of a community named Farnsburg in New York State. At some point, she was married to a man named Swift. Flora had at least four children: Eleanor and Gordon; Ruth, who had married Horace Marvin in 1896; and another daughter, name unknown, living in Hoboken, New Jersey.

In 1899, Flora, her daughter Eleanor and son, Gordon, were living in Grand Junction, Colorado. Flora was active in the Woman's Club, serving as vice-president. On June 11, 1900, the Grand Junction newspaper, the *Daily Sentinel*, reported Flora and the two children had left for a visit East. Their first stop would be Sioux City, Iowa, probably to visit her daughter and son-in-law. From there, the family traveled to Hoboken, New Jersey, for a visit with Mrs. Swift's daughter. She was still in Hoboken when her husband returned from Alaska, where he had apparently been living. He was extremely ill when he arrived and never recovered, dying sometime in late August 1900.

After her marriage to Horace, Flora Marvin settled in at Bay Meadows as the head of the household, taking care of her husband and the several family members living in Dover. When they acquired another farm, Mrs. Marvin also became involved in community activities, as she had in Colorado.

By 1900, the equal suffrage movement was active across America, pressing for changes in state and national laws to give women the right to vote. In February 1913, activists in Delaware rallied in Dover to support an equal suffrage amendment to the Delaware Constitution. A record-breaking crowd filled the State House and the House chamber, with a few select ladies of the Delaware Equal Suffrage Association speaking on behalf of the proposed bill.

On February 26, the *Evening Journal* reported Mrs. Horace Marvin spoke before the House, saying that she had lived in Colorado for several years prior to coming to Delaware. Colorado passed an equal suffrage amendment to its constitution in 1893, and Mrs. Marvin told the legislators that both she and her daughter had voted there many times.[180]

Once Dr. Marvin returned to Dover with his new wife in early 1908, he began the second, and final, phase of his move to Delaware. His original stated purpose, as told to his friends and neighbors in Iowa, and later to reporters in Delaware, was for the health of his family. Before the move, Marvin studied books and atlases on coastal places that would be healthier than the tall grass prairies of the Great Plains. On his trips to Delaware, he sought farmland he thought suitable, but unfortunately not in time to help his wife. However, there was a second purpose for his move that was only hinted at during the many interviews he gave during the previous year.

When making the decision to move East for his family, Dr. Marvin was also keenly aware he would need to have a suitable farm. In a later conversation with a Wilmington *Evening Journal* reporter who asked about his reason for coming to Delaware, Marvin mentioned that he had been a cattle rancher in Iowa. The doctor had already made a purchase of one hundred purebred cattle to be shipped to Bay Meadows, and he also planned to breed horses. They could feed on the rich summer grass in the summer and marsh hay in the winter. This would require a lot of work, but he would be assisted by his son Howard, who had graduated from an agricultural college.[181]

While Dr. Marvin was telling one reporter about raising cattle at Bay Meadows, he was telling another that, if little Horace wasn't found alive, he would return to Iowa. The farm would be given to his son Harvey if he wanted it. The doctor wasn't even going to finish unpacking the rest of his furnishings until the mystery was solved. Then, immediately after the body of Horace was found, his father repeated his intention to abandon his home and return to "live with his old friends in the west." He even telegraphed his friends in Sioux City that he would "return with Horace's body in the Fall."[182] But that was not to be.

On June 6, one month after young Horace's body was found, Dr. Marvin demonstrated his intent to remain in Delaware, at least for the immediate future. He purchased another farm property, called the Comegy farm, for $6,600. This one was sixty-five acres and described as one of the finest in the county and contained a large apple orchard and vineyard. It was located east of Dover on the road leading to Kitts Hummock, about four miles from Bay Meadows. Dr. Marvin planned to move to the new farm and resume working on a project he had envisioned before he came to Delaware while his two older sons, Harvey and Howard, would run Bay Meadows.[183]

Horace dropped out of public view for several years after the loss of his son and his marriage to Flora Swift. However, in private, Dr. Marvin was recovering his health, improving his various farm properties and becoming involved in the farming community of Delaware, making personal connections with other farmers, large and small.

In his conversations with local farmers, Marvin found common problems and a need for unity to effect changes to the high costs of getting their produce and livestock to markets. Over the course of the next two years, he joined with regional farmers to try to find a solution.

In February 1910, Dr. Marvin chaired a meeting of a group of farmers from around the state to discuss the formation of a Delaware Produce Exchange. This organization would serve as a contact between farmers and the buyers of their farm produce. By reducing the number of middlemen in the marketing chain, farmers could obtain the best market price for their goods, and the Exchange would handle the shipping and related tasks to get the food to markets around the country. This was an early version of the "from-farm-to-table" idea long before the late twentieth-century movement.

Produce exchanges had been active in the Midwest and plains area for many years, and Dr. Marvin was familiar with their operations and effectiveness. Within a few weeks, the Delaware Produce Exchange was incorporated in Delaware and offices established around the state to conduct business. In spite of initial success, by the end of 1914, the operating expenses and reduced revenue forced the Exchange to shut down.

Marvin had also been in touch with investors in Sioux City who wanted him to take charge "and join with them in a movement to secure lands in central Delaware and lay them out in fruit for modern treatment and culture."[184] Bay Meadows farm would be set out in apples and other orchard fruit in the spring of 1912, and Dr. Marvin would purchase other farms in addition to those he already owned, for the benefit of the corporation. To this end, Marvin established the Bay Meadows Fruit Company and the Dover Fruit Juice Company, being formed with a capital stock of $100,000 each and selling at $5.00 per share. Fruit packing houses and grape juice production facilities would not be built until the new orchards and vineyards were producing fruit.

The Marvins probably moved from Bay Meadows to the Comegy farm on Bay Road in late 1907. Since Bay Meadows was to be a large part of the expansion into growing fruit and raising cattle and horses, the farm would be professionally managed with Howard and Harvey Marvin's presence.

Horace and Flora appear to have stayed at the Bay Road house until early 1915. This was about the time Flora began having health problems, and the concept of the Delaware Produce Exchange had failed. The Bay Road property was sold to New York investors in May for $14,000, and both Horace and Flora Marvin dropped from public view in newspaper accounts of Kent County events.

Flora Thornton Marvin died on August 4, 1917, at their home in Camden, Delaware, after having been in declining health for several years. She was twenty-one days shy of her seventieth birthday. She was buried in Lakeside Cemetery, in Dover, near her two grandchildren.

Horace Newel Marvin died on September 29, 1918, in Dover and was buried in Lakeside Cemetery, near Flora and his two grandchildren.[185] He was seventy-three years old.

R.I.P.

Top: Headstone of young Horace Marvin Jr (*left*) and the son of Howard Marvin (*right*). *B. Cannon*. *Bottom, left*: Headstone of Horace Marvin Sr. *B. Cannon*. *Bottom, right*: Headstone of Flora Marvin. *B. Cannon*.

Acknowledgements

The author wishes to thank each of the following individuals and organization staff for their contributions to this work.

Gloria Henry and the staff of the John Dickinson Plantation Museum
Staff of the Delaware State Historic Preservation Office (SHPO)
Staff of the Bowers Beach Maritime Museum
Delaware Public Archives
Richard Marvin

James Adams   Edward Burris   Terry Graham
Susan Maclary   Bobbi Morrow   Cindy Snyder

NOTES

1. A Step Back in Time

1. Scharf, *History of Delaware*, vol. 2, *1609–1888*, 1077–79. There is a second "hummock" named Persimmon Hummock on the Delaware Bay, sixteen miles north of Kitts Hummock, at the northern end of Bombay Hook. It can be found on the Bombay Hook Island USCG topographic quad map. The GPS coordinates are 39.34033901 (latitude), -75.4871447 (longitude). The correct spelling is "h<u>u</u>mmock," but it is frequently seen as "h<u>a</u>mmock."
2. *Kent County Delaware*.
3. "A Change of Business," *Daily Gazette* (Wilmington, DE), January 22, 1881.
4. In the time of our story, these factors have not created a significant division in Delaware society.
5. "Immigrants Wanted," *Middletown (DE) Transcript*, March 7, 1907.
6. "Foreign Farm Help Must Be Well Paid," *Evening Journal* (Wilmington, DE), May 22, 1903.
7. *Religious Bodies, 1906*, 42–43.
8. *Statistical Abstract of the United States, 1907 Thirteenth Number* (Washington, D.C.: Department of Commerce and Labor, Government Printing Office, 1908). Table 13, 40.
9. *Statistical Abstract of the United States, 1907*, 249.
10. Ibid., 221.
11. *Official Guide of the Railways and Steam Navigation Lines*, 249.

12. Dr. Horace Marvin owned a Sears model car, license tag #1462; his son Horace W. Marvin owned a Stoddard-Dayton automobile, tag #1472; and brother C. Howard Marvin owned a Cadillac, tag #1355.
13. Grier, *This Was Wilmington*, 11–13.
14. *American Newspaper Directory*, 105–8.
15. *Statistical Abstract of the United States, 1907*, 64.

2. *"I Can't Find Horace!"*

16. "Marvin Case Mystery of the Age," *Evening Journal* (Wilmington, DE), May 2, 1907.
17. "Seek Water For Kitts Hammock," *Evening Journal* (Wilmington, DE), May 4, 1911. The article notes the Kitts Hummock area had been experiencing a scarcity of fresh water for years. To relieve the situation, an attempt was to be made to drill an artesian well to provide good water for those using the cottages. Being new to the area, Dr. Marvin was probably unaware of a freshwater shortage.
18. "Marvin Boy Stolen by Neighbors, Firm Conviction of Lad's Father, Who Suspects Certain Persons," *Washington (D.C.) Times*, April 21, 1907.
19. All times mentioned are standard time. The establishment of a standard for local time in the United States began on November 18, 1883, when United States and Canadian railroads instituted standard time in four time zones. Railroad time was eventually accepted and used as the general time standard in the country. There was no Daylight Saving Time until World War I.
20. The name *hundred* came to America from England, where they were units of local government and taxation. In Delaware, they were used as colonial and later state election subdivisions of counties until the 1964 U.S. Supreme Court ruling that disallowed state election districts based solely on geography. The case was *Roman v. Sincock* 377 US 695 (1964). The term is still used but only for deed registrations. It has no connection to the number one hundred.
21. "Marvin Boy Stolen by Neighbors."
22. Ibid.
23. Melanson and Stevens, *Secret Service*, 11. A Bureau of Investigations, as the FBI was first known, was established in July 1908 when President Roosevelt directed his attorney general to form a force of special agents to handle investigations referred to the U.S. attorneys in the states.

24. "Delaware Offers Reward of $2,000," *Washington (DC) Herald*, March 8, 1907, 1.

25. Ibid., 3.

26. J. Gordon Melton, "Spiritualism," *Encyclopedia Britannica*, May 3, 2013, https://www.britannica.com/topic/spiritualism-religion.

3. The Family

27. "$20,000 Offered For Missing Boy," *Evening Journal* (Wilmington, DE), March 7, 1907, 7

28. Ibid.

29. "Delaware Offers Reward of $2,000," 1.

30. "Marvin Boy Stolen by Neighbors," 5.

31. Taylor, *Handbook of the Lower Delaware River*, 33–34.

32. "Delaware Offers Reward of $2,000," 1.

33. "Marvin Boy Stolen by Neighbors," 5.

34. "Seeking History of Marvin Family," *New York Times*, March 10, 1907, 3.

35. "Marvin Boy Stolen by Neighbors," 5, 11.

36. Ibid., 11.

37. Ibid.

38. "Fates Hard on Marvin," *Evening Times-Republican* (Marshalltown, IA), April 18, 1907, 3.

39. "Marvin Boy Stolen by Neighbors," 11.

40. Delaware State Archives, RG 3555.021 Microfilm Roll 83, Deed Books, Kent County, Vol. I-9, page 347, 1906–1907.

41. "Marvin Boy Stolen by Neighbors," 6. Under English common law and in colonial America, a dower was the share of a deceased husband's real estate to which his widow was entitled after his death. In the case of Bay Meadows, a previous owner's widow had a dower interest in the property that had been passed down in the deed of every subsequent owner. So, Dr. Marvin was responsible to continue to pay.

4. Suspects

42. "Horace Marvin Alive, Kidnappers Ask Ransom," *Evening Journal* (Wilmington, DE). March 8, 1907, 1, 2.

43. Ibid., 2.

44. "Murderkill" is how the English colonizers heard the Dutch call the river. The Dutch, however, were saying "Moeder Keel" which translates to "Mother River."
45. "Kidnap Arrest Made", *Washington (D.C.) Herald*, March 9, 1907, 1.
46. "Abductors Yet Hold Little Horace Marvin," *Evening Journal* (Wilmington, DE), March 6, 1907, 1.
47. "Believe They Have Kidnappers Spotted," *Evening Journal* (Wilmington, DE), March 9, 1907, 1.
48. "Kidnapped Marvin Boy Here," *New York Sun*, March 10, 1907, 1.
49. "Missing Marvin Boy's Case Still Baffling," *Sunday Morning Star* (Wilmington, DE), March 10, 1907, 8.
50. Ibid.
51. Ibid.

5. *"Watch Murphy!"*

52. "Baby in the Hands of Child Stealers," *Evening Journal* (Wilmington, DE), March 5, 1907, 1.
53. "Drag Bay Meadows," *Washington (D.C.) Herald*, March 13, 1907, 1.
54. Ibid.
55. "Marvin Boy Is Now Believed to Be in Canada," *New York Tribune*, March 15, 1907, 3.
56. "Sure He'll Get Boy," *Sunday Morning Star* (Wilmington, DE), April 7, 1907, 3.
57. "Demand For Ransom," *Evening Star* (Wilmington, DE), March 12, 1907, 17.
58. "'Velvet Hand' Says It Holds Kidnapped Boy," *Washington (D.C.) Times*, March 14, 1907, Last Edition, 1.
59. "Marvin Boy Stolen by Neighbors," *Washington (D.C.) Times*, April 21, 1907, 11.

6. *The Trail North*

60. "Hunt Missing Boy," *Middletown (DE) Transcript*, March 16, 1907, 3.
61. "Can Horace Be Hidden in a Cave?" *Evening Journal* (Wilmington, DE), March 14, 1907, 1.
62. "Hunt Missing Boy," 3.
63. "Another Clue to Kidnappers," *New York Sun*, March 16, 1907, 4.

64. "Kidnapper Is Lured Near Marvin Home," *Washington (D.C.) Herald*, March 17, 1907, 1.

65. "Detectives Closing In on Marvin Boy's Captors," *Sunday Morning Star* (Wilmington, DE), March 17, 1907, 1.

66. "Kidnapper Is Traced," *Washington (D.C.) Herald*, March 18, 1907, 1.

67. "Kidnapper Is Lured Near Marvin Home," *Washington (D.C.) Herald*, March 17, 1907, 1.

68. Ibid.

69. "Race after Marvin Boy," *New York Tribune*, March 17, 1907, 2. At the time, Delaware's Court of Oyer and Terminer was responsible for hearing capital cases.

70. "Detectives Closing In on Marvin Boy's Captors," 1.

71. "Kidnapper Is Lured Near Marvin Home," 2.

72. "Kidnapped Boy Found by Police," *New York Evening World*, March 19, 1907, 1.

73. "Marvin Mystery More Muddled," *Kingston (NY) Daily Freeman*, March 19, 1907, 1.

74. "Aid for Boy Hunt," *Evening Star* (Washington, D.C.), March 19, 1907, 14.

75. "Erie Child Not Horace Marvin," *Evening Journal* (Wilmington, DE), March 20, 1907, 1.

76. "Wanted Marvin Boy," *Evening Journal* (Wilmington, DE), March 21, 1907, 1.

7. Advertising a Kidnapping

77. "Search For a Baby," *Middletown (DE) Transcript*, March 23,1907, 2.

78. "Baby in the Hands of Child Stealers," 1.

79. "Abductors Yet Hold Little Horace Marvin," *Evening Journal* (Wilmington, DE), March 6, 1907, 1, 2.

80. "Believe They Have Spotted Kidnappers," *Evening Journal* (Wilmington, DE), March 9, 1907.

81. Griffin, *Children's Costume*, 183; Wikipedia, "Buster Brown Suit," https://en.wikipedia.org/w/index.php?title=Buster_Brown_suit&oldid=964891733.

82. When Mark Rothko (1903–1970), a Latvian Jewish artist, immigrated to America with his family in 1913, he was wearing a Buster Brown–style suit made in Europe to hide the family's poverty and religious/cultural heritage. Breslin, *Mark Rothko*, 22.

83. "Missing Marvin Boy's Case Still Baffling," *Sunday Morning Star* (Wilmington, DE), March 10, 1907, 1.

84. "The Kidnapping of Little Horace Marvin," *Harper's Weekly*, https:// hdl.handle.net/2027/mdp.39015033848006?urlappend=%3Bseq=519.

8. The Black Hand

85. "Missing Marvin Boy's Case Still Baffling," 1.

86. "Hunt Boy in Chester," *New York Tribune*, March 22, 1907.

87. Melanson and Stevens, *Secret Service*, 34. While the agents may have been looking into some aspect of the Marvin case, such as use of the mail to commit a crime, the primary purpose of the Secret Service in 1907 was the investigation and arrest of counterfeiters of U.S. currency. Agents had been given unofficial duties for presidential protection, but the service would have to progress through years of congressional debate before its modern organization would be decided.

88. "No Real Clue Yet to the Lost Boy," *Evening Star* (Washington, D.C.), March 23, 1907, 10.

89. "Scotland Yard on the Case," *Sunday Morning Star* (Wilmington, DE), March 24, 1907, 1.

90. "Woman to Face Marvin Suspects," *Evening Journal* (Wilmington, DE), March 27, 1907, 1.

91. "Marvin Boy Found Say the Police," *Evening Star* (Washington, D.C.), March 30, 1907, 13.

92. "May Be Marvin Boy," *New York Tribune*, March 22, 1907, 2.

93. "Chases Negros with White Child," *Evening Journal* (Wilmington, DE), March 22, 1907, 3.

94. "Body Exhumed in Marvin Search," *Evening Journal* (Wilmington, DE), March 26, 1907, extra, 1.

95. "Guard Town and Seek Marvin Boy," *Evening Journal* (Wilmington, DE), March 26, 1907, extra, 1.

96. "Body Exhumed in Marvin Search," 1.

97. Ibid.

9. Here, There and Nowhere

98. "False Marvin Clues," *Washington* (D.C.) *Times*, April 1, 1907, 1.

99. Ibid.

100. "Think They Saw Boy," *Sunday Morning Star* (Wilmington, DE), April 14, 1907, 1.

101. Ibid.

102. "Dr. Marvin Has Hopes," *Pierre* (SD) *Free Press*, April 4, 1907, 1.

103. "Late News from Coast Files," *Pacific Commercial Advertiser*, March 25, 1907, 8.

104. "Kidnapped American Boy," *Whanganui* (NZ) *Herald*, May 17, 1907, 3.

105. "Offers Reward for Marvin Lad," *Evening Journal* (Wilmington, DE), April 12, 1907, 3.

106. "What Is Your Answer?" *Washington (D.C.) Times*, April 7, 1907, 2.

107. Doyle, *Sign of Four*, 93.

108. "Salvatore Antone of Hoboken Signs Demand," *Washington (D.C.) Times*, April 17, 1907, 1.

109. Ibid.

110. "Marvin Clues Prove Futile; Body a Girls," *Washington (D.C.) Times*, April 19, 1907, 1.

111. Ibid.

112. "Gloversville Police Sure They Have the Boy," *Sunday Morning Star* (Wilmington, DE), April 21, 1907, 1.

113. Ibid., 2.

114. Ibid., 1–2.

10. Butler Did It

115. "Gloversville Police Sure They Have the Boy," 1.

116. "Not Missing Marvin Child," *Daily Morning Journal and Courier* (New Haven, CT), April 22, 1907, 1.

117. "Marvin Case Near End," *Chicago Daily Tribune*, April 24, 1907, 1.

118. "Butler Arrested in Marvin Case," *Evening Journal* (Wilmington, DE), April 24, 1907, 2.

119. Ibid.

120. Ibid.

121. Ibid.

122. "Denies Killing Boy," *Washington (D.C.) Post*, April 25, 1907, 1, 3.

123. "Marvin Case Arrest," *New York Tribune*, April 25, 1907, 2.

124. "Butler Dismissed by Magistrate," *Evening Journal* (Wilmington, DE), April 25, 1907, 1.

125. Ibid.

126. Ibid.

127. "Charged with Bribery," *Middletown (DE) Transcript*, April 20, 1907, 2.
128. "Drag the Bay for the Marvin Lad," *Evening Journal* (Wilmington, DE), April 30, 1907, 5.

11. "But This Is at My Door."

129. "Horace Marvin, Probably Murdered, Found Within Half a Mile of His Father's Home," *Sunday Morning Star* (Wilmington, DE), May 5, 1907, 2.
130. "Marvin Boy Is Dead—Found by Neighbors," *Citizen-Republican* (Scotland, SD), May 9, 1907, 3.
131. "Marvin Boy Found Dead; Body in Marsh Near Home; Evidence Points to Murder," *Washington (D.C.) Times*, May 5, 1907, 2.
132. "Marvin Boy's Body Found on Marsh," *Evening Journal* (Wilmington, DE), May 7, 1907, 1.
133. "Horace Marvin, Probably Murdered," 1.
134. "Marvin Boy Found Dead near Home," *Washington (D.C.) Herald*, May 5, 1907, 1.
135. "May Exhume Body of the Marvin Boy," *Evening Journal* (Wilmington, DE), May 7, 1907, 1.

12. Questions

136. "Pathetic Scenes at Marvin Farm," *Evening Journal* (Wilmington, DE), May 6, 1907, 1.
137. "Dr. Marvin Will Leave State, Taking Boy's Body with Him," *Evening Journal* (Wilmington, DE), May 6, 1907, 1.
138. "Pathetic Scenes at Marvin Farm," 2.
139. Wikipedia, "Edmond Locard," https://en.wikipedia.org/w/index.php?title=Edmond_Locard&oldid=975673392.
140. "Pathetic Scenes at Marvin Farm," 1–2. No copies, or partial copies, of the autopsy report are known to have survived; however, a few newspaper reporters did comment on the procedure. The account given here is a composite of those reports.
141. "Marvin Boy Is Dead," 3.
142. "Pathetic Scenes at Marvin Farm," 2.
143. "Probing Boy's Death," *Fredericksburg (VA) Daily Star*, May 7, 1907, 1.

13. Judgment

144. "Sleuths Differ in Marvin Case," *Evening Journal* (Wilmington, DE), May 8, 1907, 1.
145. Ibid.
146. "Sleuths Differ in Marvin Case," 1.
147. "Arranging for Marvin Inquest," *Evening Journal* (Wilmington, DE), May 9, 1907, 1
148. "Pathetic Scenes at Marvin Farm," 2–3.
149. Ibid., 3.
150. "Ex-Coroner Has Marvin Theory," *Evening Journal* (Wilmington, DE), May 6, 1907, 1.
151. "Marvin Inquest Opens To-morrow," *Evening Journal* (Wilmington, DE), May 10, 1907, 1.
152. Ibid. In 1855, a French forensic scientist, Auguste A. Tardieu, observed small red spots, called petechiae (pet-tiki-eye) around the eyes of persons who had been victims of suffocation or strangulation. He suspected that these occurred due to the cutting off of the blood flow causing the pressure to build and the capillaries and blood vessels to rupture. In modern forensic science, these petechiae are good indicators of what may have caused a victim's death. In the case of Horace Marvin, the doctors performing the autopsy were not yet aware of this diagnostic tool. Jaffe, "Petechial Hemorrhages: A Review of Pathogenesis," 203–7.
153. "Marvin Inquest Opens To-morrow," 1.
154. Ibid. No records of March 1907 daily temperatures for Dover are known, but the last two weeks of March had noontime temperatures in Wilmington, fifty miles to the north, from the mid-40s to the mid-70s.
155. "Marvin Inquest Held in Secret," *Evening Journal* (Wilmington, DE), May 11, 1907, 1.
156. Ibid.
157. Ibid.
158. Ibid.
159. "Marvin Inquest Continued," *Sunday Morning* (Wilmington, DE), May 12, 1907, 1.
160. "Marvin Inquest Resumed Today," *Evening Journal* (Wilmington, DE), May 13, 1907, 1.
161. Ibid.
162. "Horace Marvin Died of Exposure," *Evening Journal* (Wilmington, DE), May 14, 1907, 1.

163. Ibid.

164. Ibid.

165. "Higher Milk Prices in New Jersey," *Evening Journal* (Wilmington, DE), May 16, 1907, 4.

166. A similar case occurred in New Castle on May 22, 1911, and can be found on page eight of the *Evening Journal* of that date under "River Gives Up His Body."

167. "Marvin Inquest Held in Secret," 1.

14. Epilogue

168. Based upon a search by the author of the Library of Congress, Chronicling America website, https://chroniclingamerica.loc.gov, as of November 2019.

169. The Levy Court was the elected legislative body in each of Delaware's three counties from colonial times, being responsible for raising, or levying, taxes and managing the daily operations of the county governments. As of 2020, Kent County is the last Delaware county to keep a Levy Court system, New Castle and Sussex Counties having gone to County Council formats.

170. "Pay Costs of the Marvin Inquest," *Evening Journal* (Wilmington, DE), July 3, 1907, 6.

171. "Marvin Recalled Death of Baby," *Evening Journal* (Wilmington, DE), March 12, 1908, 2.

172. "Weds Mother-In-Law," *Evening Times-Republican* (Marshalltown, IA), November 8, 1907, 3.

173. "Dr. Marvin Marries His Mother-in-Law Who Is Spiritualist," *Washington (D.C.) Times*, November 8, 1907, last edition.

174. "Dr. Horace Marvin," *Washington (D.C.) Herald*, November 15, 1907.

175. "Denies He Wed Mother-In-Law," *Evening Journal* (Wilmington, DE), November 9, 1907, 1.

176. "Echo of Marvin Case," *Evening Journal* (Wilmington, DE), December 26, 1907, 6.

177. "With Blare of Horn, Shouts and Din," *Evening Journal* (Wilmington, DE), January 1, 1908, 1.

178. "NYE History & Times Square Ball," https://www.timessquarenyc. org/times-square-new-years-eve/nye-history-times-square-ball.

179. "Dr. Marvin Weds the Mother of His Second Wife," *Evening Journal* (Wilmington, DE), January 10, 1908, 1.

180. "Women Crowd State House to Urge State Suffrage," *Evening Journal* (Wilmington, DE), February 26, 1913, 7. Delaware would not amend its constitution. The Nineteenth Amendment to the U.S. Constitution would pass the Congress in June 1919 but not be ratified by the required number of states until August 1920. Delaware would not ratify the amendment until March 6, 1923.

181. "$20,000 Offered for Missing Boy," *Evening Journal* (Wilmington, DE), March 7, 1907, 7.

182. "Dr. Marvin Will Leave State," 1.

183. "Dr. Marvin to Remain," *Evening Journal* (Wilmington, DE), June 4, 1907, 5.

184. "Fruit Farm Development," *Newark (DE) Post*, November 11, 1911, 2.

185. The Marvin plots in the Lakeside Cemetery are in the northwest corner near the triple intersection of Walker Road, North Governors Boulevard and North State Street.

BIBLIOGRAPHY

American Newspaper Directory. New York: Geo. P. Rowell & Co., 1900.

Breslin, James E.B. *Mark Rothko: A Biography*. Chicago: University of Chicago Press, 1998.

Doyle, A. Conan. *The Sign of Four*. London: Spencer Blackett, Milton House, 1890.

Grier, A.O.H. *This Was Wilmington*. Wilmington, DE: News-Journal Company, 1945.

Griffin, Irene Frances. *Children's Costume: Its Development and Stage Reproduction*. Stanford, CA: Department of Speech and Drama, Stanford University, 1955.

Jaffe, Frederick A. "Petechial Hemorrhages: A Review of Pathogenesis." *American Journal of Forensic Medicine & Pathology* 15, no. 3 (September 1994): 203–7.

Kent County Delaware. Philadelphia: A.D. Byles, publisher, 1859.

"The Kidnapping of Little Horace Marvin." *Harper's Weekly*, April 6, 1907.

Melanson, Philip H., with Peter F. Stevens. *The Secret Service: The Hidden History of an Enigmatic Agency*. New York: MJF Books, 2002.

The Official Guide of the Railways and Steam Navigation Lines of the United States, Puerto Rico, Canada, Mexico and Cuba. New York: National Railway Publication Company, 1907.

Religious Bodies, 1906. 2nd ed. Washington, D.C.: Department of Commerce and Labor, Bulletin 103, Government Printing Office, 1908.

Scharf, Thomas. *History of Delaware*, vol. 2, *1609–1888*. Philadelphia, PA: L.J. Richards & Co., 1888.

Statistical Abstract of the United States, 1907 Thirteenth Number. Washington, D.C.: Department of Commerce and Labor, Government Printing Office, 1908.

Taylor, Frank H. *The Handbook of the Lower Delaware River*. Philadelphia: George S. Harris & Sons, 1895.

INDEX

A

Allen, Alexander H. 96
Atlantic City, New Jersey 84

B

Baltimore 14, 58
Bay Meadows 34, 41, 44, 75, 90,
    119, 132, 133, 134
Bay Meadows Fruit Company 134
Bergen Point, New Jersey 93
Black Hand 49, 79, 84, 87, 92
black sloop 59
Boggle Tree Swamp 56, 104
Bowers Beach 43, 44, 79, 100, 137
Brandywine Springs Park,
    Wilmington, Delaware 53
Briggs, William H. 91
Buster Brown suit 69, 114
Butler, Frank 27, 50, 69, 83, 98,
    100, 104, 105, 107, 123

C

Caldwell, Horace 27, 50, 101, 123
Cambridge, Maryland 93
Camden, New Jersey 47
Capitol Hotel 26, 40, 63, 70, 87
Catskill, New York 96
Chesapeake and Delaware Canal
    36
Chesapeake Bay 58
Chester, Pennsylvania 62
Clark, Captain Scott "Scotty" 58
constable 29, 32, 51, 52, 93
coroner's jury 108, 109, 111, 117,
    126
Court of Oyer and Terminer 62

D

Delaware Bay 11, 15, 16, 26, 27,
    30, 35, 106
Delaware City 42, 46

Delaware Equal Suffrage
    Association 132
Delaware legislature 14, 30, 88
Delaware newspapers 18
Delaware Produce Exchange 134
Delaware River 15
Dover and Philadelphia Navigation
    Company 99
Dover, Delaware 11, 26, 75, 131
Dover Fruit Juice Company 134

E

electric service 17
Erie, Pennsylvania 64

F

Federal Bureau of Investigation 31

G

Gloversville, New York 97
Grand Junction, Colorado 132
Grand Jury 94, 98, 104

H

Harper's Weekly 73
Hart, John 43
Hawaii 89
Henze, William (hermit) 79
hobo 92
Hoboken, New Jersey 92
Holmes, Sherlock 91

Home for Friendless and Destitute
    Children 57
Howard, A.P. (Erie attorney) 65
hummock 12
hundred 29
Hutchinson's Cave 56

I

immigration 14

J

John P. Wilson (steamship) 99

K

Kent County 11, 15
Kent County Court House 116,
    124
Killen, Lucy 83
Kitts Hummock 11, 12, 13, 15, 16,
    18, 24, 38, 62

L

literacy rate 18
Little Creek 11, 16, 36, 40
Logan School 25, 82
Lore, Frank (New Jersey State
    Detective) 61

M

Magnolia, Delaware 43, 79, 83, 116
Maritime Reporting Station 36
Marriage Bureau, New York City 131
Marvin, Dr. Horace, Sr. 26
Marvin farm 19, 21, 24, 25, 42, 43, 44, 49, 60, 83, 86, 91, 93, 105, 106, 111, 112, 121, 123
Marvin, Harvey 65, 88, 128, 134
Marvin, Horace, Jr. 26, 39, 51, 63, 69, 84, 86, 107, 109, 111, 113
Marvin, Horace Newel, III 128
Marvin, Howard 101, 128, 131
Marvin, John 26
Marvin, John Swift 39
Marvin Reward Postcard 76
McQuade, Thomas (Pittsburgh Superintendent of Police) 48
Mechanicsville, New York 52, 85
Middletown 17, 18
Milford 17, 79, 121
Murderkill Creek 43, 44
Murphy, Frederick 32, 52, 93, 96, 97, 106

N

New Castle 17, 38, 43, 46, 47, 100, 125
New Castle County 14, 15, 16, 17, 106, 114
New Haven, Connecticut 97
New Year's Eve 1908 130
North Somers Point, New Jersey 84

P

Philadelphia 15, 44, 76
Philadelphia Maritime Exchange 36
Pinebird, Joseph 62, 130
Pinkerton 31, 42, 48, 51, 59, 79, 80, 81, 94, 99
Pittsburgh, Pennsylvania 48
Pleasanton, Frank 57
Pleasanton, Ollie 43, 44, 107, 118
population 15
Portsmouth, England 82
post offices 16
Proudfit Mystery, the 125
public roads 16
public safety 29
public water systems 21

Q

Quarantine Station 36

R

railroad 15
Rankin, Pennsylvania 48
ransom 37, 48, 50, 53, 65, 87, 90
Ratledge, James 56
Reedy Island 15, 42
Richards, Robert H., Attorney General 31
Roma 80
Roosevelt, Theodore Jr. 14, 80
Ross, Charlie (1874 Philadelphia kidnapping) 87

S

Secret Service 31, 80
Sheldon Detective Agency 50
sheriff 30
Sioux City, Iowa 26, 39, 128, 132
Smith, Elsie 57
South Camden, New Jersey 52
South Norwalk, Connecticut 88
Spencer, William 76, 89
spiritualism 32
Standish, Miles 26, 35, 62, 68, 70,
       89, 96
Standish, Rose 26, 32, 59
state detective 30, 56
St. Jones Creek 43, 100
straw stack 24, 32, 35, 49, 50, 58,
       60, 98, 101, 112, 123
Swift, Flora M. 26
Swift, Ruth 39

T

Tannebaum, Charles 50
telegraph 17
   first message around the world 17
telephone 17, 30, 59
Thomas, Rufus 58

V

Velvet Hand, the 53
Verden, Frank 27

W

Wagner, Edward (Erie Chief of
       Police) 64
Wesley Methodist Episcopal Church
       55
Whanganui, New Zealand 89
Wharton, John 57
Wilmington Methodist Conference
       55
Woodall, Charles 21, 27, 34, 40,
       60, 101, 102, 123

ABOUT THE AUTHOR

Brian Cannon is a Delaware native with family connections back to early Dutch and English settlers. Living in Delaware, he developed his love of history while growing up hearing family stories, as well as local myths and legends. After serving in the U.S. Air Force, he had a twenty-year career in fire protection and safety management in the insurance industry. Following retirement, he had the opportunity to work for the State of Delaware at the New Castle Court House Museum, retiring as the lead interpreter after twenty-two years. In this position, he developed numerous presentations on Delaware history, plus two plays, and New Castle town and veteran's walking tours.

Visit us at
www.historypress.com